A Systems Approach to Education and Training

Edited by A. J. Romiszowski

Kogan Page

These papers were originally presented at
the conference "Systems Approach to Education and Training" which was organised
jointly by the Association for Programmed
Learning and Educational Technology, and
by Enfield College of Technology, and which
was held at Enfield College of Technology
on September 18th 1969.

Published by Kogan Page
16 Grays Inn Road, London WC1

Designed by Edna A. Moore
Printed in Great Britain by Express Litho Service (Oxford)
SBN 85038 230 0

PIC

The Programmed Instruction Centre (PIC) is based at Enfield
College of Technology, Queensway, Enfield, Middx, and exists to
promote the use of programmed methods and materials - in the
widest sense of this term - within the college courses, in the schools
of the Local Education Authorities, and also in industrial and com-
mercial concerns throughout the British Isles.
The Centre writes programmes for industrial and college use,
trains programme writers, engages in research and development
projects on a co-operative basis with schools and industry, and acts
as an information and advice centre.
It has also acted in this instance as host to APLET and as
organiser of the "Systems Approach" conference.

APLET

The Association for Programmed Learning and Educational Technology (APLET) is a voluntary body which exists to promote the
development and use of efficient methods of instruction in education
and in training. It produces a research journal "Programmed
Learning and Educational Technology", (published by Sweet and
Maxwell), a monthly newsletter "Programmed Learning News"
(which appears as part of the magazine "Visual Education"), and
organises an annual conference which attracts a wide selection of
papers and delegates both from Britain and from overseas.
More recently a policy of supporting short, single topic, one-day
conferences has been adopted. The "Systems Approach" conference,
the source of this symposium of papers, was one of the first of
these short conferences to be organised.
The new address of APLET is 33, Queen Anne Street, London W1.

Contents

NOTE: The paper by the service officers from the Navy
is published with the permission of Her Majesty's
Stationery Office.

Foreword

During the international Conference on Programmed Learning and Educational Technology, which was held at Goldsmith's College, London from 11th to 14th April 1969, a working party was formed to investigate the "Systems Approach". This group, about sixteen strong, set itself the following objectives:

a) to survey the interests of the members of the group.
b) to reach a consensus view of the systems approach and clarify some of the terminology used.
c) to show how the systems approach may be applied to real-life situations.
d) to discuss possibilities for further communication on this topic.

Objectives b) and c) were only partly met during the conference, so the realisation of objective d) became particularly important. This commenced by circulation of some papers among the members of the group, and a paper summarising the discussions at the conference was prepared by M. MacDonald-Ross.

As interest in this topic grew, a need for further meetings developed. Thus, in line with the APLET policy to encourage regional one-day conferences, a conference was arranged at Enfield College of Technology to deal specifically with the theory and practical application of systems approaches to education and training.

This conference was held on September 18th 1969, and attracted nearly 100 delegates, an indication of the increasing interest in the topic. A further indication has been the large number of enquiries for copies of the papers delivered, received from people who were unable to attend the conference. It was therefore decided to edit and publish the papers delivered in order to make them generally available.

This process has taken some time, due to various problems. Some changes have occurred in the practical applications described in some of the papers. For example, the Open University is by now very much further ahead in its planning and the organisational systems described here are now worked out in greater detail. Similarly the centre of activity in the Royal Navy has moved from Scotland to the South of England, and work is again progressing to a more advanced stage. Finally, due to the protracted illness of one of the contributors to the conference, this symposium unfortunately lacks one of the papers originally delivered.

However, in general, this selection of papers clearly indicates the present "state of the art" regarding systems approaches to education. It is not intended as a treatise on the systems approach. Indeed the reader will discover that there is not just one single interpretation of this term. He will be able to use the references appended to the papers to follow up the various theoretical approaches if he so wishes. He will however gain from this symposium an insight into the general principles of a "systems approach" and an overview of the practical applications which are currently being attempted.

A J ROMISZOWSKI
Conference Organiser and Symposium Editor
Enfield College, June 1970

Systems approaches to education and training
An introduction

by A. J. Romiszowski   Enfield College of Technology

"A system is a little black box,
Of which we can't unlock the locks,
But find out what its all about
By what goes in and what comes out. . ."

The term 'system' has been used in many ways by many people.
Similarly, the perhaps more recent term 'systems approach' has
been used in at least three senses by writers on the subject. To
some a systems approach to education implies the use of educational
hardware; closed-circuit television, teaching machines, film projectors. Others draw parallels between the precise functional
objectives used by the systems engineer and the programme writer's
behavioural objectives; between model building and task analysis or
course synthesis; between simulation and validation. Thus they
define the systems approach as the application of programmed learning principles to all aspects of a course. They would claim that the
systems approach is a scientific approach to structuring courses (2;
3) Finally, still others would reserve the term 'systems approach'
to describe the application of cybernetics to the teaching and learning
processes. This implies a rigorous, probably a mathematical
approach, which considers the teacher and learner interaction as an
adaptive system, susceptible to the same forms of control as, say,
animal nervous systems. Such an approach may lead to the construction of mechanisms which simulate part of the system, for
example "SAKI" or the Rank "Talking Typewriter". (4)

It is not surprising therefore, that still others see the whole concept of systems and 'systems approach' as a new jargon, which has
been conjured up to explain old ideas; invented (or at least promoted)
by those who wish to obscure that they are substituting talk for
action.

The one-day conference on the Systems Approach which was held
in September 1969 at Enfield College of Technology, was organised
by the Association for Programmed Learning and Educational Technology in conjunction with the college, in order to investigate further

the various meanings ascribed to this new concept, to try to clarify some of the jargon which has arisen, to review work of a practical nature which has been done in attempts to apply a systems approach, and finally to discuss the limitations of systems approaches in the field of education.

What is a System?

In this context, a system is an inter-relation of parts. For example, a bicycle is a simple system, although it is composed of quite a large number of separate parts, each one having a specific function. The parts and their functions are inter-related to each other in specific ways, so that together they perform adequately to achieve the purpose of the system as a whole, that is, to move the rider from A to B.

We could, however, also regard the bicycle and the rider on it as one system. In this particular case, various inter-relations exist between the rider, his limbs, and various parts of the bicycle. It would seem, therefore, that to a certain extent we could regard anything as a system, provided that we define its boundary, that is, that we circumscribe the parts which do make up the system that we are interested in. In practice, of course, the boundary which we choose for our system is very often defined for us, or is self-evident. For example, if we were considering the mechanical construction of a bicycle, we would probably not consider the rider as part of the system, but rather consider the way that he affects the bicycle, i.e. by his weight, by the force he exerts on the pedals or by the steering he applies to the handlebars. We consider these as INPUTS to the system from outside, i.e. from the environment in which the system operates. On the other hand, if we were considering the dynamic balance of a bicycle when cornering at speed on a racetrack we might consider the rider and the bicycle as one and the same system, and consider the way that it impinges on its environment, i.e. the track, and the way that the track affects the system.

Thus we see that any system has a boundary which we must define and locate. Within this boundary there is an assembly of parts or elements which are in some way or other inter-related or dependent upon each other, and it also has an environment made up of all the things outside the boundary. Finally, the environment and the system interact as well. We refer to inputs to and outputs from the system. Figure 1 illustrates schematically this concept of a system.

Of course the elements A, B, C, D within our schematic system may be capable of further sub-division into parts, and thus form SUB-SYSTEMS.

Types of Systems

The example of the bicycle illustrates a type of system where although there are several parts (perhaps quite a lot of parts) coll-

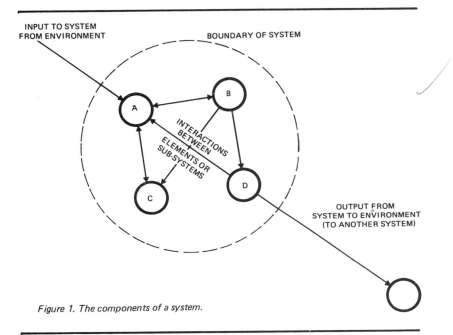

INPUT TO SYSTEM
FROM ENVIRONMENT

BOUNDARY OF SYSTEM

INTERACTIONS BETWEEN ELEMENTS OR SUB-SYSTEMS

OUTPUT FROM
SYSTEM TO ENVIRONMENT
(TO ANOTHER SYSTEM)

Figure 1. The components of a system.

ected together and inter-related in some way or other, the inter- ·
relations are quite predictable, and can in fact be determined in
advance, by means of simple mathematics. The example of a
system composed of a bicycle plus the human being, if we are considering this system in the environment of a race track, may no
longer be quite so easily determined. We may not with full confidence be able to predict exactly how this system will behave if the
environment takes on certain parameters. For example, if another
cyclist falls off in front of our particular system, we may not be able
to predict exactly what avoiding action our rider will take, although
we may perhaps be able to predict with some level of confidence that
he will probably take a particular type of avoiding action because of
the particular position (or what have you) of the accident.

We see therefore two types of systems: Deterministic - ones
which can be determined in advance, where every inter-relation
between every part can be prescribed, and providing that the system
continues to function and does not break down, we know exactly how
the system will behave at any particular time and under any influenc-
es from the environment; and secondly Probabilistic systems, that is
systems where we cannot be certain on how the total system will
behave under certain conditions of the environment, although we can
in some cases be fairly confident about the type of reaction which
will take place.

13

	SIMPLE	COMPLEX	EXCEEDINGLY COMPLEX
DETERMINISTIC	WINDOW CATCH WORKSHOP LAYOUT	DIGITAL COMPUTER AUTOMATION	
PROBABILISTIC	TOSSING A PENNY STATISTICAL QUALITY CONTROL	STOCK EXCHANGE DEALINGS CONDITIONED REFLEXES	THE ECONOMY THE BRAIN THE COMPANY EDUCATION AND TRAINING

Figure 2. A classification of systems.

Systems may also vary in the sheer complexity of the inter-relationships which exist, and in the sheer number of elements which are inter-related. For example, a motor car is a much more complex system than a bicycle, with more or less the same function or purpose, but although it is more complex the inter-relationship between the various mechanical parts of the car may still be predicted in a deterministic fashion. At the other end of the spectrum the window catch has only one moving part and one fixed part, but can also be regarded as a system with a specific purpose and again is obviously deterministic. Similarly, probabilistic systems may be simple or complex. For example, tossing a penny a hundred times may be thought of as a system, the output of which is a number of heads or of tails which are achieved. We cannot exactly predict how many heads we will achieve, so this is obviously a probabilistic system. It is quite simple in its structure. Stock exchange dealings are much more complex in their structure, and it is much more difficult to predict with great accuracy the outcome of a particular deal. Finally, we have the total economy of the country, the human brain, animal nervous systems, company organisations, and indeed education and training, all of which are highly probabilistic and also so complex that they really defy complete specification. Figure 2 shows a classification suggested by Stafford Beer for classifying systems according to their type (1). Such a classification is useful because it identifies the sort of techniques which may be used to try to investigate a particular system. The techniques for investigating deterministic systems are different from those which are necessary for investigating probabilistic systems, and similarly the techniques for investigating a simple system like tossing a penny are very different from those which will be required to try to investigate the working of the human brain. Although exceedingly complex probabilistic systems defy total definition, there are nevertheless techniques which may be used to study these systems, and indeed to control their operation. These techniques spring out of the science of cybernetics, and we shall be returning in several of the papers to look at how these techniques may be applied to education.

Educational Systems

There are two ways in which the term "educational system" is used.
a) In the traditional sense. We refer to the British educational system. We are usually here referring to the system of provision of materials, resources etc. The boundary of such a system is defined to include all the educational institutions which are implied by the title. For example, the British educational system would include, we presume, all educational institutions and organisations working within the country, while a state educational system would include within this boundary only those schools and colleges for which the state is directly responsible. The environment of the educational system is the society in which the system flourishes; the jobs, the culture, background etc. The basic input to the system are people (learners) although there are subsidiary inputs in the form of resources which may take material form, or money, or indeed again they may be human resources in the form of teachers. The major output from the system is again people, but people at a different, presumably higher, level of "education".
b) We also now hear the words "educational system" used in the programmed learning sense. We refer to "educational", or "teaching", or "training", or perhaps best of all "instructional" systems. In this concept the boundary of the system includes little else but the learner himself. The environment, is his school, the society and the various resources available to the learner. The inputs to the system are information which may be transmitted to him by various methods or media, and the output is the learner's performance. The papers in this symposium deal with both of these basic models. The paper by Dr. Neill on applying the systems approach in The Open University and the paper by Peter Hodge on applying systems approaches in school organisation, both deal with an educational system with a precisely defined boundary and precisely defined sub-systems within the boundary. The papers by Gordon Pask, by Edgar Stones and by the Royal Navy deal with attempts at the implementation of

"instructional" systems. Nevertheless, there are vast differences between the approaches used by these authors. These approaches differ in the extent to which they use theoretical models simply at a conceptual level, or the extent to which they manage to quantify or mathematically define the inter-relationships which exist between the elements in the system. As Neill and Hodge refer to them in their papers, the models that one constructs of the system may be iconic (that is, simply a schematic representation of how things hang together and interact) or they may be more or less mathematical and quantified. The papers in this symposium show both of these approaches. It may be useful before moving on to look at these two distinct types of systems approach a little more closely.

Systems Approaches

We will first discuss the sort of systems approach which is to all extents and purposes an extension of the principles of programmed instruction to the programming of total courses irrespective of the methods and media used for their presentation. This historical development of programmed instruction, the basic principles, and the way in which it has grown into a total systems approach is outlined in the paper of Professor Frank George. It will suffice here to simply summarise the characteristics of this approach. Several models for this type of systems approach have been proposed in the literature. The one reproduced in Figure 3 is suggested by Derek Rowntree (2). Similar models, differing in detail are suggested in the papers of E. Stones and the contribution from the Royal Navy. We see that the process of course construction follows a series of stages very similar in their aims to the stages which are followed when instructional programmes are written. We notice also that at several points in this procedure, feedback loops exist, which suggest that earlier stages in the course construction are reconsidered and revised in the light of new information. This is an important characteristic of the systems approach. Although Figure 3 and the other diagrams presented in the symposium seem to imply a sequence of stages in course construction, these stages are in fact very closely inter-related, and although one may start by specifying objectives before writing the syllabus, one will inevitably reconsider the objectives while writing the syllabus and so on. Thus the process is really a cyclic, recirculating one. By studying Figure 3, one can however identify three major types of activity which do occur at various points in this model. Firstly, there are stages of analysis. Analysis of the trainee himself, and analysis of the subject matter. The results of the analysis stages are presented as a set of training objectives. Secondly, there are the stages of synthesis of a solution to the problem (in this particular case the construction of the course).

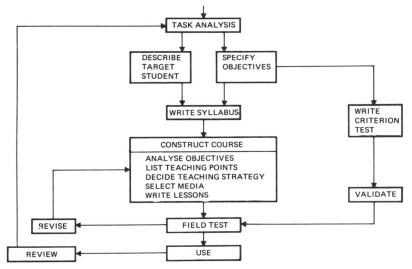

Figure 3. The 'SYSTEMS APPROACH' to the design of courses or lessons.

Thirdly, there are the stages of evaluation when the course materials (the end result of the second stage) are measured against the training objectives (the result of the first) and any necessary improvements are carried out. Rowntree (2) makes the analogy between these three stages involved in systematic course construction, and the stages involved in scientific method. He equates the task analysis stages to identifying a problem, the synthesis stages to the postulation of a hypothesis, and of course the evaluation stages to testing the hypothesis to see whether it holds true. In this sense therefore this particular definition of a systems approach can be thought of as a scientific method of course construction. However, it must be noted that the techniques often used in practice in carrying out the analysis and synthesis and finally the evaluation are not always entirely scientific in themselves. This is not intended to be a criticism of the practitioners of the systems approach but rather an indication of the lack of objective techniques in course design available to us at the present time. This point is made particularly strongly by Lt. Commander Stevenson in the Royal Navy's contribution to this symposium. He outlines an attempt to maximise the objectivity of the decisions taken during the task analysis stages and the course construction stages.

The second type of systems approach discussed in the papers of this symposium is an approach which is based thoroughly on general systems theory, or cybernetics. Cybernetics is an interdisciplinary

17

approach to problems of control and organisation in exceedingly complex probabilistic systems. We have already seen that education and training in all its aspects is certainly in this category. One interesting finding in cybernetics is that many of the problems associated with complex systems of this sort may be dealt with by the same techniques irrespective of the type of system. We are implying that techniques which may be developed to investigate, measure or control an animal nervous system, or a country's economic system, may also be applicable to the investigation and control of an educational system. The stages in applying an approach based on general systems theory may also be categorised as stages of analysis, synthesis and evaluation. However, the result of analysis would normally be expressed as a model: a model describing the system as it exists and the inter-relationships which exist between the elements. The result of the synthesis stages will again be a model. This will be a model of the solution, the new system if you like, and the new inter-relationships which are to exist. Finally, of course, evaluation would involve testing this new model to ascertain whether it indeed solves the problems which it has been set up to solve. Over the past few years a number of formal techniques have sprung out of cybernetics and related studies which enable some of these stages to be carried out in a scientific and objective manner. For example, to enable us to carry out analysis the tools of formal logic, statistics, information theory and operational research have been developed. To aid us in the synthesis of model solutions, certain basic concepts such as the "variety" of a system and "entropy" in a system, have been developed. And finally, the evaluation of our model may be carried out not in real life (which may be both lengthy and expensive, particularly if the model is faulty) but by simulation techniques on computers, so that we may in advance evaluate whether the model is worthy of being put into practice.

We are probably quite some way from applying this sort of systems approach to total educational systems at the national or international level. One problem is that we do not know at present how to quantify the perameters which control the functioning of our system, nor indeed can we specify all the perameters which are relevant. However, on a smaller scale, attempts are being made to apply this sort of approach in education. The papers of Dr. Neill and Peter Hodge describe attempts to apply general systems theory to closely prescribed educational systems. Peter Hodge's paper is also useful in having as its preface a glossary and quick definition of some of the jargon terms which have arisen out of cybernetics systems theory. In the paper of Dr. Gordon Pask we have several examples of successful applications of cybernetics approaches to specific training tasks which can for various reasons be relatively easily analysed and the various inter-relationships existing within the system quantified.

However, in his paper Dr. Pask points out that it is not perhaps
necessary to be able to quantify every parameter within a system in
order to be able to control and predict its behaviour. In his intro-
ductory paper, Professor Frank George outlines some of the basic
principles of cybernetics, among them the useful concept of the
"black box".

The Black Box
Three main characteristics of cybernetics systems theory seem to be
particularly relevant to educational systems. Firstly, educational
systems are nothing if not probabilistic. We therefore need statistics,
information theory and all the other techniques we can muster in
order to try to control and predict them. Secondly, educational
systems have a purpose; to produce human beings with certain skills,
knowledge or attitudes which will fit them for the society in which
they live. The inputs in terms of information content must be controlled in order to achieve the required outputs. This control is
achieved by a process of feedback, or homeostasis. Cybernetics
deals specifically with a study of how such feedback may be rendered
effective and efficient. Thirdly, and in the long run perhaps most
importantly, cybernetics has given us the concept of the black box.
This is a concept which enables us to regard a system, or a sub-
system within a system, as a totally enclosed unit (black box) which
has certain inputs into it and outputs from it. We may be able to
define how the outputs will vary if we vary the inputs in a particular
way, and we may indeed be able to control this process, but to do
this we may not necessarily ever have to know exactly what goes on
within the black box. In other words, we have here a method of
overcoming the problem posed at the beginning of this paper, the
problem of educational systems being in effect so complex that they
defy ever being completely defined in every detail. The black box
concept means that we need not in fact ever define them in detail.
We simply need to link the input and output by appropriate parameters.
This approach which is used by Pask and is described also in the
paper by Hodge, holds out vast promise for the control of education
in the future.

Implications for Education
We can probably regard the two types of systems approaches outlined above really as two ends of a continuum. We start with the
loosely defined iconic model where we are unable to quantify the
inter-relationships between the various sub-systems which make up
our educational or training system, but as our techniques improve
and we are able to quantify we are driven closer and closer towards
a "general systems theory" based approach to educational problems.
At the present point in time, we are able, as demonstrated by the

papers of George and Pask, to construct cybernetic training systems to deal efficiently with very specifically defined training tasks. It would be not unreasonable to assume that it is only a question of time, and particularly of money spent on research, before greater and greater areas of education and training may be subject to a similar type of treatment. It may be still a long time before we are in a position to, for example, construct a model of a British educational system based on the concept of comprehensive education, run this on a computer, modify the various inputs from the environment (that is the social system) and predict whether the particular form of comprehensive education we are now adopting is indeed going to solve the problems which it is designed to solve. We may be even further away from being able to implement scientifically the sort of major re-organisations to education which the philosophers are currently predicting to be necessary. The models for "education for the 21st century" which are being suggested by educationalists (for example, the concept of "permanent education" as outlined in various surveys and research reports commissioned by UNESCO the Council of Europe, OECD, and various American agencies (5)) would imply vast re-organisations in the total pattern of education within the industrialised world. The exact form of any such vast re-organisation, which certainly seems to be necessary if we are to maintain and improve our standard of living, is critical. The present techniques of political control of the education offered within a society are completely antiquated, in the light of the speed with which change is progressing in society in general. The traditional methods of feedback or homeostasis which operate at the moment within education are suitable to a very slowly changing, almost static, feudal type of society as indeed existed during the Middle Ages. Change in the inputs to our educational system was effected over the generations by changes in attitude and a change in needs slowly filtering back. We now experience more change within one generation than we used to get within several centuries. It would not be unfair to say that the major problem in education at the moment is the lack of homeostatic control, the lack of effective feedback. The only source of such feedback which looks promising is the application of techniques of control and prediction based on the science of cybernetics.

Thus although at the present time the systems approach may quite validly be considered in most of its applications as simply an up-grading of programmed instruction, it is likely in the long run to become the backbone of change in education. It may not be too pessimistic to suggest that unless developments take place in the science of cybernetics and in its application to education, we will face a situation where an industrialised society is peopled by a race culturally and intellectually incapable of controlling its environment.

It is for these reasons that I attach particular importance to this symposium of papers. Although they illustrate only a scattering of work in the field, they do at least indicate the beginnings of an interdisciplinary approach - an approach which relates education with the society in which it takes place, and attempts to do this in a scientific rather than intuitive manner.

It remains only at this stage to thank the contributors for the papers which they have prepared and their kindness in delivering them at the joint APLET/ECT Conference last September.

References

1 BEER, S
   Cybernetics and Management, English University Press, 1959

2 ROWNTREE, D
   The Systems Approach
   In: Yearbook of Educational and Instructional Technology 1969/70
   Cornmarket Press

3 DANIELS, A
   Practical Applications of Educational Systems in Industry
   In: The Systems Approach to Education
   Audio-Visual Media, Autumn 1969
   Pergamon Press

4 NEIL, M. W
   Escape from Inertia - An Application of a Systems Approach to Learning
   In: The Systems Approach to Education
   Audio-Visual Media, Autumn 1969
   Pergamon Press

5 Permanent Education - An Agent of Change in the Present Education System
   Council of Europe, Studies in Permanent Education No. 6 (1969)

Educational technology
The systems approach and cybernetics

by Professor F. H. George Brunel University

First of all, let me be clear that by "educational technology" I mean
the various methods and techniques that have been evolved for the
transmission of information from person to person, in particular
from a teacher to a student. There is a whole world of possibilities
involved including computers, overhead projectors, films, television,
radio and the rather especially important field of programmed
instruction.

As far as this particular paper is concerned, I shall talk in terms
of programmed instruction as being representative of the whole field
of educational technology. The reason for this is partly because I
cannot possibly deal with all the different techniques which have been
developed in one short talk, and partly because programmed instruction seems to be a central, perhaps the central, contribution to the
current state of technological development in education.

I could reasonably call this the field of Educational Cybernetics.
Cybernetics is concerned with control and communication in animals,
men and machines, and is especially concerned with the field of
artificial intelligence. The application of this to various aspects of
society makes up collectively the field of applied cybernetics. Some
well-developed fields of applied cybernetics already exist such as
Bio-cybernetics, Behavioural Cybernetics, Social Cybernetics,
Mathematical Cybernetics, Industrial Cybernetics, including automation, and here in this paper we will be discussing Educational
Cybernetics.

The implication is that Educational Cybernetics will eventually use
the methods of artificial intelligence to either simulate or synthesise
the human teacher and provide, as a result, a completely flexible
and wholly adaptive type of teaching system. I shall waste no time
in discussing the various implications of this and its close association
with what is sometimes referred to as heuristic programming. Rather
I shall get straight to the main point which is the extent to which we
can approximate, at this moment in development, to the wholly
flexible ideal of the humanlike intelligence, or its artificial equivalent or superior, being used as a teacher.

It should also be remembered that we are concerned with the systems approach to education, and by this I take us to mean very much what we mean by Educational Cybernetics. We mean, in other words, to emphasise the dynamic, the changing, the adaptive and the evolutionary features of our system. Society changes and changes at an increasing rate, and we should expect that all the systems that try in some measure to simulate or synthesise and help social needs should themselves possess all these various features of change. These features of change should be represented by feedback, both positive and negative, as well as feed-forward. *

We can say at this stage that one of the discouraging features of our existing educational system, good as it is by world standards, at both the level of school and university, as well as all the other associated educational institutions, including business and industrial education, is that it is of the last century. It emphasises, albeit unconsciously, static features of our surroundings rather than the dynamic ones which are the ones which are the most important; the ones which are becoming increasingly obvious and becoming more and more in need of understanding and control. I shall be discussing a little bit later the context in which programmed instruction, as a representative of educational technology, is likely to occur and develop. In the meantime, I would like to say a little bit more about programmed instruction itself.

I PROGRAMMED INSTRUCTION
Ia Its Development
Programmed instruction is a means of representing information flow, in an adaptive way, from teacher to student. Even the classroom situation with a human teacher has relatively little feedback, because questions and answers do not occur for much of the time. This means that the human teacher has to rely on expressions and reactions of the students with only the occasional questioning or testing of their understanding of what has occurred. Motivation too is difficult to sustain in this particular type of context, where a human teacher may repeat year after year the same sort of information and almost inevitably has a decreasing interest in whether or not the information is being understood and properly utilised.

Programmed instruction then aims to provide the information feedback by means of question and answer. There are many different ways in which this may be done and I shall be devoting a few separate statements to the questions of the actual medium, the way the information processing is planned, and the style in which the programme is ultimately written. In the meantime, let me say simply

* See paper by Pask for examples. (Ed.)

that we may use teaching machines, of various kinds, and we may use information processing in various ways. What is central to all the media used and all the methods employed is that it all depends upon feedback.

Programmed instruction historically has been thought by some to go back a very long way indeed. In fact, it is no coincidence that two of the largest computer controlled programmed instruction installations (C.A.I.) in the United States are called SOCRATES and PLATO. The idea of question-and-answer as a means of propagating information and obtaining the feedback which is necessary to confirm that the information has been understood is by no means new.

In recent years there has been a fresh interest shown in programmed instruction. In 1926, S. L. Pressey was the first person in the moden era to make small machines with questions and answers, of a multiple choice kind, leaving the student to select the answer he chooses from a number of possible alternatives. This has for a long time been a popular technique for use in examinations, part-icularly.in the United States of America, but Pressey here was using what was essentially an "examination technique" for instruction. It is clear indeed that in testing someone one is also informing them in some measure. Generally speaking, however, one feels there is a distinction to be made between the passing of information and the testing to make sure that information has been properly acquired. The overlap occurs, precisely because in testing, and then supplying the correct answer, one is doing, if in the less desirable order, the same thing as passing on information in the first place; both methods are valuable, and stand among a whole host of other methods that are suitable for use in the programming context.

1b Fabric of Programmed Instruction

We have already indicated that our question and answer methods, with all the possible variations that can occur, can be transmitted in almost any sort of fabric. You can have teaching machines which look like television sets, or slide rules or packets of postcards or even rolls of paper in a small box.

The very fact that teaching machines can look like a collection of postcards is a reminder that books themselves can be programmed. Indeed, of course, it is questionable whether a packet of postcards with a box in which they can be slid up and down constitutes a teaching machine or constitutes a type of book; the two things easily grade into each other.

It is also possible to use television as a medium for programmed instruction. The difficulty is that an auxiliary book or some form of test, perhaps by telephone, is necessary if the feedback feature is to be maintained where television is the stimulus medium.

It goes without saying that programmes do not need to be purely visual – whether pictorial or in the written word – they can also be auditory or even appeal to the other senses, or any combination of those senses.

Teaching machines can be both simulatory as well as descriptive, and it is natural that if you were teaching a physical skill, such as handling equipment of a more or less complicated kind, or even learning physics or chemistry or biology in the academic milieu, then one would expect to have to use equipment independent of the machine although controlled by it. We use the word 'machine' here as taking care of the whole field of programmed instruction whether in book or in alternative hardware form.

There is therefore no restriction on the fabric, although when the fabric is chosen there is some restriction on the way the material can be processed. Some machines impose heavy constraints on the alternative questions that can be asked, if alternatives are required, whereas others impose very few constraints indeed. In fact, in the case of a book, the constraints imposed over such issues as the number of alternatives is far less than is imposed by the logic of the situation. This means that the hardware constraints become unimportant.

1c Planning

One of the things about programmed instruction that is most beguiling is the relative ease with which the programmes seem to be able to be written. Once they have been written, however, they have to be thoroughly tested, checked and validated. This means that they have to be shown to be efficient at processing information in the actual context in which they are to be ultimately used. When these checks have been carried out, it becomes quite clear that the process of writing such programmes is by no means as easy as it seems.

The upshot is that as much time, if not more, has to be spent on organising the material and carefully planning the programme as is spent in actually writing the words that make up the information and formulate the questions and answers.

The process required is exceptionally complicated and we are not in a position to say with certainty exactly what are the necessary and sufficient conditions for effective programming at this moment in time. However, among the various techniques used, that of flow-charting, which is very similar to that of systems analysis in computer programmes, is necessary. In fact, there is a very close analogy between the use of the computer and computer programming and the use of the teaching machine and teaching machine programming.

In the planning of the programme, there are many things that have to be considered, among them are such questions as the order of the information flow, the amount of practice with particular examples,

25

the careful establishing of certain vital concepts necessary to an understanding of the total material, the amount of practice which the student will need in order to make sure the concepts are fully understood, and so on and so forth.

Once more one has to admit a degree of ignorance as to the best ways of representing information for various different types of people, age groups, etc. We know only a few general principles which seem to stand us in good stead and which we can check and test and improve on as the result of experience.

Id Style of Programme Writing

Under the general heading of "style" we should point out that having planned the programme and having planned the method by which we try to instruct the student, we still have the problem of actually writing the frames.

In a sense the question of the organisation of the material and the style in which it is written overlap. This is so, because we may, among other possible views, take a deductive or an inductive, an historical or a fictional approach, a linear or a branching technique. But whichever method we choose to adopt, the style in which we write should be appropriate to the mode of approach as a whole. Style is one of the ways in which motivation can be introduced into the learning situation. Unless motivation is present, it is very difficult for the student to retain that which is important in the material since, of course, retention is a vital feature of all learning.

There still remains a whole host of questions to be asked and answered about the proper processing of information in educational modality. We know something about the nature of whole versus part methods of processing material. We know that where the material is highly meaningful, the whole method, up to a point, is better than the part. Thus it is that children tend to retain poems better if they are learned as a whole rather than if they are learned on a line-by-line basis.

Similarly, "spaced" learning is probably more efficient than "massed" learning. In other words, a child who learns to play the piano on a five minutes a day basis learns a great deal more efficiently, in general, than if the thirty-five minutes of the week were all in one continuous session.

There are many other features such as interference, transfer of training, concept formation, short-term and long-term memory, rehearsal, etc., which we need to understand more fully, and associate with different types of people and different concepts, before we can lay down any hard and fast rules about the nature of the "ideal" programme.

Because we do not fully understand how to write an ideal programme, we should not for a single moment suppose that programmed instruction is not already a vital and viable part of information processing, because it certainly is. Even some "bad" programmes teach effectively if used in the right context. This really represents the fact that motivation and the other features which make for learning are independent in some measure of the actual information processing itself.

II THE CONTEXT OF EDUCATIONAL TECHNOLOGY

In this section I would like to draw attention to the general context in which programmed instruction and other techniques of educational technology are most efficiently used. We must start by asserting once again that our existing educational system is rigid and static in outlook and almost wholly outdated in method. The notion of class-room teaching is itself out of keeping with our understanding of how information processing can be most efficient. It is quite impossible, in general, for any one teacher to pass information across to a group of students at a rate which appeals to the learning ability of each equally efficiently. This argument will be further expanded in the next section, but even a simple experiment with an existing school form or class illustrates well the individual differences that are suppressed by group teaching. Given programmed instruction as a method of teaching, the individuals in the class soon show themselves as quite different in their rate of learning in respect to different subjects. The objection raised to this point by the teachers and administrators in the school is that this disrupts the whole organisation of the school. The answer to this is that it most certainly does, and this is highly desirable, because what is in effect taking place is the removing of a straight-jacket from the school's activities.

All of this suggests that with the advent of computer assisted instruction, the computer will be as much used in organising the school work as it will in actually helping to process information handled by terminals plugged into the computer.

In trying to search for a set of principles for showing that these sorts of educational methods can be made viable, it is clear that some sort of neo-Dalton plan is necessary. People learn best when they teach themselves; they learn best principles rather than facts; they learn best when they participate with the other features of their environment; they learn best when they understand the purpose for which they are trying to get the information in the first place.

All these principles could be made to apply to traditional educational activities, but in practice they normally do not. It is very much easier for a person, if properly organised, to acquire precisely the information he needs for some specific purpose than it is if he merely tries to pick and choose, often without sufficient guidance or instruction, from that information which is presented to him willy-nilly. It is being suggested that there must and will be a transform-ation in our educational methods in the future. If this transformation is to take place smoothly, it will almost inevitably be based on the principles of, and employ many of the techniques of cybernetics.

III CYBERNETICS AND ITS RELEVANCE TO EDUCATION
IIIa Cybernetics - is the science of control on communication.
Norbert Weiner (the founder) said that it applies equally to animals, men and machines. The main implication is of course that you can construct machines in the laboratory which have more or less the same abilities as have human beings, or at least hold out the prospect of such. Therefore it is not surprising that the fundamental problem in cybernetics is thought of as that of artificial intelligence. It is the central issue we are confronted with and what we attempt to do is to show that we can manufacture such systems "artificially". By "artificially" one might mean at one end of the scale that we construct some device from wheels and cogs, and at the other end that we, as it were, produce a "seed" and grow our system in the laboratory. The first is crude to say the least, the second is extremely difficult though it may indeed be possible in the future. So in fact we settle for something different altogether - we ask ourselves what is a sufficiently large-scale system, preferably already available, which will allow us (in a reasonably short, economical period of time) to build a system which has some measure of complexity comparable to the human being - and inevitably therefore we get landed with the digital computer. The only reason that we are "landed" with it is that it is the only available universal machine. Until a program is put in it, it does not have any activity at all. A child would be in the same position if unfortunately you forgot to put in his program - the nervous system.

One can think of a computer therefore as something not precisely and completely defined. You can write a program to fit into it which will make it do anything that your ingenuity enables you to put into the program in the first place.

Now the most important thing in this field of artificial intelligence, is that we attempt to put into the computer something which is self-programming. Hence one disposes of the view that the programmers are the people who matter and the programme (and therefore the computer) only does what it has been programmed to do.

Of course there is a stage in which computers only do what they are programmed to do, in the way that human beings also only do what they are "programmed" to do. But the point is that you can program computers to interact with their environment in such a way that they learn from experience. They accumulate information and one could say that this (however much more abstractly, however much more limited by hardware, language etc.), is an analogy of the social intercourse between humans.

Humans interact with other humans. Computers interact with

computers, and as we disapprove of apartheid computers interact with humans.

There is no reason why, theoretically, we should not generate artificially the same type and level of intelligence as exists in humans. Many cyberneticians, myself included, believe that we will be able to in practice generate the same level of intelligence as human beings and indeed exceed it, - because if you do understand the principles that allow you to even get to the same level, you can probably use the same principles to exceed it. I cannot think of any reason for supposing that human intelligence is some sort of limiting variable, like the speed of light, which could not in principle be exceeded. However, I have no wish to provoke philosophical controversies, and will proceed to outline how this way of thinking is influencing education.

IIIb Educational Cybernetics

Cybernetics breaks down into a number of sub-disciplines. Social cybernetics, mathematical cybernetics (this is concerned with the mathematical methods used - stochastic processes, Markov nets, mathematical logic), bio-cybernetics, (making biological models, simulating neural nets) behavioural cybernetics (making models of human behaviour, particularly of the cognitive aspects), industrial cybernetics (models of industrial systems, automation, organisation and methods), and education cybernetics - the one we are primarily concerned with here.

We should make one other distinction. In the cybernetics field we are concerned with both SIMULATION and SYNTHESIS. By simulation we mean copying human behaviour - using biological models as a guide to the formation of your blueprints. We are concerned with the same methods and the same ends as existing human or animal behaviour, though we would be manufacturing our model out of different materials.

In synthesis however, we are concerned solely with the ends and not the means. We are not concerned at all whether our automation works in the way that humans do, as long as it achieves the ends of providing an artificially intelligent system - able for example to plan, make decisions or solve problems. It could be argued that this is an artificial distinction - that one never considers ends without considering means, and that inevitably one is led to consider the means used by oneself. However it is a useful distinction. For example various methods have been devised by people to recognise shapes, colours, patterns etc. in the environment. There are many different processes that can be used. It is unlikely that all these methods exist in the human sensory system. Some of them may exist, but not all. Therefore when attempting synthesis, one may also be attempting simulation, but not necessarily so.

What is there in cybernetics that has any bearing on educational activities? One is that of course cybernetics aims to provide models or principles which refer to any system whatever. Secondly, the attitude adopted to education should be influenced by cybernetics. Here are some terms used in cybernetics which help to illustrate my point.

Adaption, Feedback, Evolution

People are in evolution. Societies are in evolution. The system society builds must therefore also evolve. One of the means of providing evolution is adaptation. Adaptation to changing circumstances is often achieved through feedback (knowledge of results).

One major criticism of the educational system as it exists at the moment, is that it does not evolve, at least not until recently, and certainly it does not evolve fast enough. It seems that the educational system of this country, and indeed any existing educational system, has not realised consciously the need to evolve as circumstances change. One of the features of our system is the installation in people of the belief that things do not change all that much. Indeed we build in a resistance to change: why change if we are winning; if it was good enough for my father it is good enough for me; it has always been done that way.

There are signs however over the last 10 or 15 years that at last educationalists are realising that the old systems don't work, that there is a need for change.

One main development which highlights this trend, and which points the way to change, is the emergence of a widespread acceptance of programmed instruction. Programmed instruction I regard as the main theme among a number of themes which, although not strictly cybernetics, represent the result of a cybernetic type of thinking. For example, we are slowly getting away from the idea that only human beings can teach other human beings. I have often heard it said in the past that the ideal educational system could be one individual tutor for one individual pupil. I cannot think of a more ludicrous example of an ideal educational system. Anybody who has been submitted to this process knows that it is absolutely and totally unbearable. Nothing could be more boring than having one person all the time worrying about what you are learning. One big advantage of a teaching machine when used in this sort of situation is that you can at least switch it off.

Almost as ludicrous is the classical educational pattern of classrooms of 40 or more pupils being instructed by one man at the front, in the belief that there is nothing quite like the human contact between teacher and pupil. There may be nothing like it, but that does not mean it is good or efficient. Of course personal contact is required, but not all the time, or for all aspects of a subject equally. Students need to participate actively in the learning process, they need to interact with their environment. The way in which this can be best achieved will depend very largely on the characteristics of the topic being learnt, and also on the individual student. Certainly for much routine learning - of facts, techniques, even principles - systems involving machines may often be the ideal answer. But education is more than information processing, and the broader issues of making people suitable for the society in which they live (in as much as we know how to do this at all) is best done by human beings.

So I don't think that Programmed Instruction, or any of the other technological aids which are now being used, are in themselves a solution to any of our educational problems, but the very use of them as parts of teaching systems does show that something has rubbed off on teachers from the work and the way of thinking of cyberneticians and systems engineers.

Of course there is still resistance - partly because people do not want to be bothered to learn new tricks, partly because various teaching aids and systems, even when available are not designed for easy use. However, this should not obscure the general fact that we must make optimum use of every available aid if we are going to make our education genuinely of the 20th Century.

One of the problems encountered by sponsors on novel methods or media in education has always been to get teachers, schools and local authorities to use them. One of the reasons for this is that you have to re-think your total organisation to accept them. It is very much analogous to buying a computer. If you install it and then use it just as a peripheral device, another helpmate, .then you are using it uneconomically and stupidly. The fact is you have to change the methods you used in the past to fit in with the computer - to meet the computer half way. This is the same in educational technology. This involves one in considering the system as it exists, in re-thinking the system, in considering alternatives.

In one study carried out in several European countries, it appeared that the most limiting, and most artificial factor in most systems is the idea of classrooms and fixed length sessions. Another weakness in most educational systems is the examination structure. Hence the current experiments in individualised instruction, in project-centred work, in inter-disciplinary studies, and in continuous assessment. Also the trend in research is now to investigate, not one particular technique, but rather which techniques are suitable for a particular type of learning.

This brings me to another weakness of the present educational system - the type of learning demanded. In studies of learning, and indeed of examination passing, we find that successful students do not concentrate on learning vast quantities of facts, but rather they learn the principles involved, together with a minimum quantity of

facts. Even so, current course and examination structures require
students to learn more facts than real life problems ever require.
Hence the current trends in curriculum studies - the new mathematics
for instance.

All these current trends involve one in looking at education as a
complex system. They involve techniques of analysis, of synthesis,
and of evaluation. As such they draw from cybernetics, if not many
actual techniques at present, then at least an approach, a way of
thinking.

IIIc Computers and Heuristic Programming

Now the greatest future influence on the educational process in terms
of hardware, is likely to be the digital computer. At present, most
computer-assisted instruction applications use algorithmic programming methods, that is a precise procedure is laid down, each
step is taken according to a pre-determined set of criteria, alternative routes through the material to be learnt are pre-planned and
inflexible. The complexity may be much greater but essentially the
strategy is similar to that used in traditional branching programmes.

But of course the point about human beings, and therefore also
about artificial intelligence systems, is that they hardly ever behave
algorithmically. They are generally heuristic. This means that they
make jumps, guesses, take short-cuts, they set up hypotheses and
then test them.

The use of a fixed, algorithmic procedure is by far the exception
rather than the rule in human activity. Of course it is desirable
and economic to use in some applications (e.g. aircraft maintenance
where absolute precision is aimed for), but in many cases it is not
economical, as the decisions which have to be made are so numerous.
In many other cases it is impossible. There is no algorithm for
forecasting future demand in business, and there is also no algorithm
for saying how you should teach a child.

Therefore, I believe, that much of C.A.I. of the future will be
based on heuristic methods of programming - methods which do not
lay down a fixed procedure, but allow for adaptation to a particular
situation. In short (and perhaps somewhat misleadingly) we must
aim at the simulation of the good human teacher. This will involve
us in making the characteristics of the good human teacher absolutely
explicit. When this is done, we should be able to construct heuristic
programmes to simulate these characteristics.

It is these heuristic methods, rather than the currently used
algorithmic ones which are the particular concern of cybernetics. This
particular notion of heuristic programming is more directly involved
than any other in the construction of artificial intelligence.

Not only can computers be used to teach heuristically (by simulating real teachers' characteristics) they can also manage a school or

an organisation heuristically. The Neo–Daltonian schools of the future, with widespread individualisation of learning, pose new problems for the organiser. The present system has been running for centuries and still we have not ironed out many problems, despite constant experimentation and changes in approach. This is because the problems of such complex systems are insoluble – we can at best implement a change and then evaluate it. With heuristic programming we can simulate that change, and in a short period of time, evaluate the probable outcomes before committing ourselves irrevocably to a new policy.

The economic viability of constructing vast, heuristically programmed systems, either for C.A.I. or for school organisation and management, has been challenged. This may be so at present, but certainly great developments in the economic realisation of such systems are being made, or are just round the corner. Among those of paramount importance is the production of cheap (perhaps chemical) computer stores. The amount of data to be processed by heuristic programming methods is generally vast, so cheap stores are essential. Another development of great relevance is the progress in computerised editing, typesetting and printing. By these methods one can typeset a book of 600 pages in 9 hours. These methods can also be used for the preparation and printing of programmed units, notes and individual instructions to students.

These are the sort of developments which may help to make C.A.I. a reality, no longer just a dream. The underlying science which guides these developments and which will increasingly guide their application, is the science of cybernetics.

Applying a systems approach in the Royal Navy

I Introduction

by Instructor Lieutenant Commander R.E.B. BUDGETT, RN
We are seeing today much evidence of the way in which involvement
in Programme Instruction leads to involvement in overall Training
Systems. This is also the experience of the Royal Navy; we have
found it inadvisable to consider programming subject matter in iso-
lation. In the Royal Naval Programmed Instruction Unit we now
recommend that a whole training scheme should be looked at system-
atically and only when a particular learning requirement is seen in
its relationship to the whole should the effort be spent on programming it.

A Naval Training Establishment which is looking at its committ-
ments in this light is the Naval Air Station at Arbroath in Scotland.
Lieutenant Commander STEVENSON, is from the staff of this station
and it has been his task to put our recommendations into practice.
As an air engineer, who is also a pilot, his operational task is to
test fly aircraft squadrons after pre-issue maintenance, but he is now
taking his turn in a training establishment and providing the necessary
feedback from the operational world. Lieutenant Commander Stevenson
will be describing his experiences of starting up a Training System in
the last though larger part of this paper.

Before attempting to put the system into practice it was necessary
to train Lieutenant Commander Stevenson and his team. This was
done in the Royal Naval Programmed Instruction Unit, of which
Lieutenant Commander MORSE, is the Training Officer. He is a
Canadian – the benefit of whose North American experience we have
been glad to have for the last year. He will explain briefly our
philosophy in this matter and the way in which we suggest it should
be put into practice.

II In theory

by Instructor Lieutenant Commander S.L. MORSE, Canadian Armed Forces
The Royal Naval Programmed Instruction Unit has the responsibility
of ensuring that personnel selected for training in the Unit will apply
the best available methods and techniques as they endeavour to develop effective in-service training programmes. The increasing

complexity of operational equipment, the rapidly changing personnel requirements and the expanding store of new training methods and techniques available to the trainer demanded that we provide him with a practical process by which he may direct and control training development and implementation i.e. make it possible for him to effectively manage his students' learning. The principle activities in such a process are:

(a) data gathering;
(b) decision-making;
(c) documentation for communication between various levels of training management; and
(d) training evaluation.

As instructional programmers we recognized that programme development consisted essentially of the same activities, but at a lower management level (1, 2, 3). It was discovered that the Systems Approach to Training advocated by several writers claimed to do for training in general what the highly disciplined procedures so familiar to instructional programmers had proven to do for Programmed Instruction in particular. The urgent need for a guiding concept for use in training personnel to view training design in a more critical manner naturally led to adoption by the Unit of the Systems Approach. The Conceptual Model which we have used is not original for many similar models have been proposed by others and we have borrowed heavily from existing literature in its design (4, 5, 6, 7, 8, 9, 10). I will represent it simply in terms of the eight stages of documentation required with the need for supporting data and the critical decision points being implicit within each stage.

Stage 1.   Determination of Operational Requirements in detail by Job Analysis.

Stage 2.   Determination of Skill and Knowledge elements demanded by operational requirements by task analysis and specification of student population characteristics.

Stage 3.   Derivation of Training Objectives expressed in student performance terms together with applicable performance conditions and standards in accordance with Mager (11).

Stage 4.   Specification of Criterion Measures to be used to check on student achievement of derived training objectives.

Stage 5.   Synthesis of Training Design Documentation in the form of lesson specifications and procedures, programmed instructional materials, training aids, etc. considered relevant to the objectives derived. Incidentally all media and strategy decisions are held in abeyance until this point in the sequence, including decisions regarding the employment and/or development of programmed instructional materials.

Stage 6. Implementation of the Programme in accordance with the training strategies decided upon.

Stage 7. Presentation of Validation statistics in terms of student achievement of the training objectives for assessment of effectiveness of training strategy.

Stage 8. Provision of Evaluation data to check relevancy of derived objectives. In essence this means checking to see whether or not students, who have achieved the training objectives, are able to perform effectively in the operational environment. Provided the operational requirements have remained the same, inability to perform on the job at this stage would strongly suggest that the objectives need adjusting. Figure 1 portrays the Systems Approach to Training as we envisage it with the two "feedback" loops

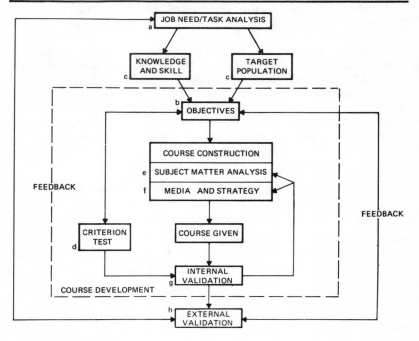

Figure 1. CHECKS

1. The check that the course meets the objectives is carried out by the internal Validation (includes Criterion Test).

2. The check that overall training meets the Job Requirements is carried out by external Validation.

which are so essential in ensuring that the system will be adjusted for error as required.

In view of the experience we have had in the development of training objectives in many areas of Naval Training, it would be in order to comment further about their function in the training system. While we have subscribed whole-heartedly to Mager's original design to ensure clarity of training intent (11) we have felt that he did not emphasize clearly enough how important it was to ensure the relevancy of the objectives set. He has more recently appeared to recognize this shortcoming and has now clearly supported the value of task analysis procedures in the establishment of relevance (4). In fact his model for developing vocational instruction is similar to the model described above. Several other writers have emphasised the merit of task analysis in deriving meaningful training objectives (12, 13, 14, 15). The stress we place on objectives stems from our conviction that they are the vital link between the operational and training requirements - a link which has not always been accorded the emphasis we place on it in the approach being described here. It is our contention that this failure in the past has led to ineffective training design because many critical decisions have been made subjectively.

A logical question at this point would be, "How does this beautiful concept work out in the cold dawn of practical training design?" Lieutenant Commander Stevenson will conclude the presentation by describing the experiences of his team as they struggled to implement the Systems Approach to Training as it was presented to them.

III In practice
by Lieutenant Commander P.M. STEVENSON, RN

FOREWORD

I represent the Royal Naval Mechanical Air Engineering School at Arbroath in Angus, HMS Condor.

The task of CONDOR is the training of skilled and semi-skilled ratings of the Fleet Air Arm in the maintenance and repair of Royal Naval aircraft, ashore and afloat.

In January of 1969, I was directed "to administer the programming of the Naval Air Mechanics Course". The Naval Air Mechanic is the most junior of the semi-skilled mechanical engineering Fleet Air Arm ratings, the equivalent of an Aircraftsman in the RAF. His course is one of many which is undertaken at CONDOR, and lasts for 15 weeks.

A team of two Aircraft Artificers 1st Class was nominated and a preliminary two-day acquaintance course given by Lieutenant

Commander Morse at CONDOR. This was followed by a full two week course of Programme Writing at HMS Collingwood, which I also attended.

During this course, we evolved a plan of attack, under the guidance of Lieut. Cdr. Morse and, for practice in Programme writing techniques, wrote three short programmes about aircraft mechanical systems.

During the discussions about our approach to the problem we realised that the Programming of the Naval Air Mechanics course in its entirety was not possible but also undesirable.

It was decided that the prime need was to establish the Course Training Objectives before considering programming. I believe that, in the past, attempts at complete course programming have failed because established syllabi have been taken, in toto, without considering their validity. I further believe that there are few courses in existence which have established their training content entirely objectively. They have generally been established over a period of time by the introduction of bright ideas and personal prejudices sometimes based on need, sometimes not. In specific training it is only cost effective for the trainee to learn material which is directly related to the JOB.

JOB DESCRIPTION

We therefore had to write a detailed Job Description for the man we intended to train, the Naval Air Mechanic. Because of a recent Service requirement, there was a Job Description available for this rating. However, on close study it was found to be inappropriate for our needs. It was, perhaps, adequate for the assessment of the man's worth by the Prices and Incomes Board, but it was certainly not adequate to define the beginning of a Job Analysis, with a course of training in mind. Fifty percent of it was expressed in terms of basic or working knowledge. I defy any two people to agree in the requirements of skills and knowledge needed, to define basic or working knowledge. We therefore decided to write our own Job Description. This was not difficult, because all of us have recently employed the Naval Air Mechanic, and his tasks are well defined by our Aircraft Publications and Maintenance Manuals.

It was written on five sheets of foolscap close typed, and entirely in objective terms as defined by Mager (11). The JOB was stated in 16 working areas, covering 168 specific tasks.

TASK ANALYSIS

The systems model used for the Task Analysis of the Job Description was based upon that outlined by Gibson and Morse (10) but the approach was modified considerably by the subject matter. The 168 tasks were each expanded in separate booklets of either 4 or 8 pages, depending on the complexity of the task. The main task was stated on the title page of each booklet, with reference to relevant publications and tools required. The remainder was in tabulated form: columns entitled "What to Do", "How to do it" and "Key Points". Now, what do we mean by these terms?

1. What to Do (or Sub-task) Every operation required by the trainee to achieve the specific task.

2. How to do it Any expansions of the sub-task required due to the complexity of even the sub-task or the requirement of specific skills.

3. Key Points A list of all points of association, skill, knowledge or understanding required to achieve each sub-task to the required standard.

I would like to point out at this stage that throughout the analysis a very strict accounting procedure was employed. At each expansion, particularly at the later stages, it would be only too easy to lose some of the analysis components because of the vast amount of paper work involved. The accounting was covered in two ways:

1. By annotating each component of the analysis as it was used for the next stage, and ensuring that all components were so annotated before proceeding further.

2. By producing an alphabetical Key Point Index which had the further advantage of showing where emphasis lay in areas of required knowledge which were common for different tasks.

We now had 168 booklets containing everything that the Naval Air Mechanic is required to DO, and everything that he is required to KNOW. Each booklet was assessed in the following way.

1. In Importance of Teaching Each Sub-task/Key-Point was given a numerical assessment of 1 to 6, ranging from "Vital for Safety" to "unessential background".

2. In Teaching Difficulty Each Key Point was graded in teaching difficulty, ranging from "Very Difficult" to "No Further Training Required".

3. In Supervision Each Task was graded "Un-supervised", "Partially supervised" or "Fully Supervised".

4. In Performance Each Task was assessed in the five terms of performance defined by Mager (4).

From the results of our task analysis, we could at this stage see the beginnings of a Course. The priorities of the course were beginning to make themselves apparent. The Sub-task/Key Point association which is difficult and important to teach, unsupervised, involving problem solving and discrimination, clearly has priority over an easy to teach, relatively unimportant, fully supervised task involving, say, recall.

From the beginning, the team had maintained a time chart to give some idea of the cost of the project. At this stage, the time which had been spent by my two analysts was 360 manhours

TERMINAL OBJECTIVES

From the previous analysis, Terminal Objectives were stated. These came straight from the Task Analysis booklets, with the following extracted:

1. Sub-task/Key Point associations, which would be learnt by formal field training.
2. Sub-task/Key-points which were considered to be learnt adequately by experience in the field.

It is noted that this extraction was carried out subjectively to a certain extent, but was based on our personal practical knowledge of the man's operational employment.

They covered 46 more sheets, each containing from one to six statements of achievement required of the Naval Air Mechanic when he arrives at his first unit. These can be equated with the Gibson and Morse (10) classification of Class 2 Objectives.

The terminal objectives were regrouped and expressed as criteria in Mager (11) form of Task, Standard and Conditions where-ever possible. The standard and conditions are, in the field, generally implied by aircraft publications and known Service environments. Because we were expressing objectives for a training environment, Standard and Conditions had to be modified, to an extent.

ENABLING OBJECTIVES

Enabling Objectives were now extracted from the mass of Key-points, and arranged in preliminary training areas, which were mainly selected for convenience at this stage of synthesis, purely to "see the wood for the trees". They covered nearly 100 sheets of foolscap. These were then re-arranged and re-written in the form of a Provisional Syllabus, having two parts:

1. Enabling Objectives or course content.
2. Terminal Objectives or criteria, covering both practical and written aspects.

The total time taken to reach this stage was 720 manhours.

The provisional syllabus was issued to those sections in the Training Department at CONDOR which would be directly involved in the adoption of the new course. They were asked to give constructive criticism about accuracy of information, omissions and superfluities. I limited the criticism to within the context of the course that we had defined. I did not want pre-conceived ideas to get into the system from the previous traditionally evolved syllabus, however good that was. It was considered apt to consult the proposed users of the course at every stage from now on, but to control their influence. I believe that failures in course programming have occurred in the past because programmers have tried to impose a course method onto a teaching staff who are unable to accept or understand its principles or derivation.

With the background of our analysis, there could be no argument about the validity of the subject matter, except perhaps in emphasis. However, it is, I think, essential to employ the experience of long-standing teaching staff to advise on areas of difficulty.

No mention of a Pre-test has yet been made. At CONDOR, we are supplied with a rating whose ability is well defined by the Selection test he undergoes. In this, he has to achieve a minimum level of simple Mathematics and English. It may be found necessary to derive pre-tests or gate-tests later, but this is not envisaged at present. Anyway, our target population is pretty well defined for us by recruiting procedures.

After the Section criticism, the syllabus was re-written having been modified in:
1. Some of the subject area teaching order.
2. Some of the subject matter accuracy.
3. The removal of some mutually agreed superfluous items.
4. The addition of a few items which were justified by the established teaching staff, after discussion.
and it was produced in a 4 Phase format:

1. Non Technical Phase   It was considered necessary for the establishment of the right frame of mind in the trainee, to give him the necessary motivation. This phase has no criterion test, and was evolved entirely subjectively.
2. Technical Phase   covering all the enabling objectives.
3. Consolidation Phase   Consisting of revision of the Technical Phase in conjunction with the achievement of some Terminal Objectives, while under direct instruction or supervision.
4. Criterion Phase   The Terminal Objectives of the course in two sections:
   a. Written
   b. Practical

The re-written syllabus was then discussed at higher administrative level to iron out any disagreements between my team and the users. It is noted that throughout the discussions the general principles were never the subject of conflict. Arbitration was only needed in minor points of detail.

TRAINING METHODS AND AIDS
Training methods were discussed at Instructor level to decide which subjects merited programming, and which should be learnt by Chalk and Talk, Overhead Projection, Film or Practical methods. Naturally, we found that a great deal of the subject matter of the traditionally evolved course and the syllabus that we have produced is the same. We did not want to Programme for programming sake, and we considered that if traditional methods have proved to have no failings at all, then traditional methods should still be used. Also, we certainly did not want to programme subject matter which is likely to change in the foreseeable future. However, even for the traditionally taught subjects, I considered that it was necessary for my team to control them tightly by the production of standardised lesson plans.

Having established the training method Training Aid requirements were agreed and listed. The supply of these is being arranged.

PROGRAMMES AND LESSON PLANS
The team has now been supplemented by one rating instructor for the writing of lesson plans, while the two original members of the team have now started to write the first programmes. The policy on which we have agreed is to incorporate the new syllabus item by item, as each lesson plan or programme is completed. This will involve the gradual change from the existing examination and testing methods, to the Criteria we have defined.

It is difficult to say how long this will take, but I hope that the incorporation of the complete course will be achieved within a year.

I must emphasize here, that we have no validation of the system model yet, and we will not have this proof of the pudding for eighteen months, but we have a product, albeit not an end product, but something that is usable.

We cannot yet say whether the course length can be reduced from 15 weeks, but we have the satisfaction of knowing that all that is taught, based upon this syllabus, will be relevant in every way to the man's operational employment, and a true basis for further training.

The foregoing has been achieved in 1200 manhours.

I believe that this will be of interest regarding the cost of the system.

LEADING AIR MECHANICS
We can now see an end product of the Naval Air Mechanics course, but the Naval Air Mechanic is only one grade of rating involved in aircraft maintenance. The Mechanical Air Engineering School for the Fleet Air Arm deals with many different ratings both skilled and semi-skilled. Our next task was to carry out an analysis of the Job of a Leading Air Mechanic. He is one rate up from the Naval Air

Mechanic, and the equivalent of a corporal in the Royal Engineers, or the Royal Air Force. He has a more responsible job involving limited supervision of Naval Air Mechanics and is required to carry out jobs needing more experience and more background knowledge that the Naval Air Mechanic.

JOBS DESCRIPTION

The statement of the Job Description of a Leading Air Mechanic is not so straightforward as that of the Naval Air Mechanic, and we decided to carry out market research on the use of our product. In a book on management I read recently, a statement caught my eye as particularly relevant: "Frequently a manufacturer is surprised at the difference between what he intended his product to be used for and what it is actually used for". With the Naval Air Mechanic, there was no doubt as to how he was going to be used, and we are manufacturing trained Naval Air Mechanics. We are also training Leading Air Mechanics on a 10 week course and it has been long believed that the course could be reduced in length. We wanted to find out what our product was being used for before thinking of the evolution of a course. A team went around the Naval Air Stations questioning Leading Air Mechanics and their employers on what they actually did, not what people thought they did or what they ought to do. This was done by tabulating every task that the Leading Air Mechanic was expected to carry out over and above the job of the Naval Air Mechanic. We called this a Difference Job Description. The result of this survey was factual confirmation of long held opinions that the present course was not completely realistic.

The result of this survey also gave us a factual starting point for analysis.

Because the course is a supplement to the basic Naval Air Mechanics course, based on a Difference Job Description, and also because of our accumulated experience, the analysis process has not taken as long as that for the Naval Air Mechanic. In about 150 Survey Team manhours, we have achieved the statement of Training Objectives for the Leading Air Mechanics course.

I believe that this is invaluable for us, for we will no longer be teaching doubtful subject matter. It is anticipated that the installation of the analysis-based course for Leading Air Mechanics will take place well before that of the Naval Air Mechanics, as it is intended that, for the moment, conventional teaching methods will be employed. What it has shown, however, is that the course can be reasonably reduced from 10 weeks to about 6, and yet still give adequate time for the ratings assessment for further skilled training.

PETTY OFFICER AIR FITTER

The Petty Officer Air Fitter, the equivalent of a Sergeant in the Army or Royal Air Force, is the next in line for survey. A team is in the field carrying out a systematic confirmation of the Petty Officer Air Fitter's Job Description. This is again more complicated than that for the Leading Air Mechanic, as the Petty Officer Air Fitter's responsibilities are far greater, because he is employed in a fully supervisory status. Again we are aiming for a Difference Job Description between the qualified Petty Officer Air Fitter and the qualified Leading Air Mechanic to define the limits of our course.

SUMMARY

What have we achieved in 6 months at CONDOR?
1. By analysis, we have produced a Naval Air Mechanics' syllabus, agreed by both analysts and users, and have progressed to the stage of programme and lesson plan writing.
2. By field survey and analysis we have achieved Training Objectives for a course for the Leading Air Mechanic.
3. We have carried out the preliminary planning for a field survey of the employment of the Petty Officer Air Fitter.
This has been achieved in 1400 manhours total analyst and programme writer employment.

REFERENCES

1 MELCHING, W. H
The Text of an Orientation Workshop in Automated Instruction
A Consulting Report, Subtask TEXTRUCT II
Fort Bliss; Texas: US Army Defence Human Research Unit, 1962

2 LYSAUGHT, J. P and WILLIAMS, C. M
A Guide to Programmed Instruction
New York: John Wiley and Sons Inc, 1961

3 Programmed Learning - Airforce Manual No. 50-1
Washington: US Government Printing Office, 1967

4 MAGER, R. F and BEACH, K. M
Developing Vocational Instruction
Palo Alto, California: Fearon Publishers, 1967

5 THOMAS, D. B
The Application of a Systems Approach to Instructor Training
RAF Education Bulletin No. 5, (Autumn 1968) pp 3-10

6 DAVIES, I. K
The Management of Learning
RAF Education Bulletin No. 4, (Autumn 1967) pp 24-33

7 CRAWFORD, MEREDITH P
   Concepts of Training, in Psychological Principles in System
   Development
   Edited by R M Gagne, New York: Holt, Rinehart and Winston, 1963

8 ECKSTRAND, G. A
   Current Status of the Technology of Training
   A Technical Report AMRL - TR - 64 - 86. Prepared for Behavioural
   Sciences Laboratories
   Air Force Systems Command, Wright Patterson Air Force Base,
   Ohio, September 1964

9 SMITH, ROBERT G, Jnr
   The Design of Instructional Systems
   A Technical Report 66-18. Prepared for the Department of the Army,
   Washington: US Department of Commerce, 1966

10 GIBSON, A. H and MORSE, S. L
    Application of Instructional Technology to the Training of Personnel
    in the Canadian Armed Forces,
    Paper presented at the International Conference of the Association
    for Programmed Learning and Educational Technology, April 12,
    1969, London, England

11 MAGER, R. F
    Preparing Instructional Objectives
    Palo Alto, California: Fearon Publishers, 1964

12 MCGEHEE, W and THAYER, P. W
    Training in Business and Industry
    New York: John Wiley and Sons Inc, 1961

13 GAGNÉ, R. M
    Presidential Address
    Division of Military Psychology of the American Psychological
    Association as cited by Robert G Smith Jnr
    Programmed Instruction and the Technology of Training in
    'Trends in Programmed Instruction' edited by G B Ofiesh and
    W C Meierhenry
    Washington: Department of Audiovisual Instruction and the
    National Education Association, 1964

14 MORSH, JOSEPH E
    Job Analysis and its Application to Training in 'Trends in Programmed
    Instruction' ibid

15 LATTERNER, CHARLES
Task Analysis - Bane or Blessing in 'Trends in Programmed
Instruction' ibid

EDITOR'S NOTE

The Naval Air Station, HMS CONDOR, at Arbroath was closed in
1970. The Naval Engineering School transferred to the Naval Air
Station, HMS DAEDALUS at Lee on Solent, where the work
described in this paper continues.

Practical applications of cybernetics to the design of training systems

by Dr. Gordon Pask Systems Research Ltd.

Cybernetics, as you know, is the science of control, communication and information. How does this definition apply to the general area of psychology and in particular to training and education? I cannot hope to cover this topic in a single short paper. What I will try to do is to pick out a few isolated sub-topics which we can look at and then to give a few examples of how attention to these topics has been of practical use or might be of practical use.

I MODELS AND MODULES

First of all I would like to concur very heartily with Mr. Edgar Stones* in laying emphasis on modules. At the present state of the art we do know quite a bit about how certain educational sub-routines should be managed, and what constitutes good teaching strategy in these cases. For example, in the case of language learning the case of teaching people to perform transformations let us say from the negative to the affirmative or from the singular to the plural. This would be an area sufficiently narrow for us to approach it by 'plugging in' a model for learning (which would essentially be a cybernetic model) and which would allow us to evaluate what was going on with respect to this particular skill. For we can carry out an evaluation with respect to a well defined model; without one, we cannot do so.

Now the same sort of comment applies to teaching somebody a keyboard skill, or teaching somebody to control a machine, or to a part of the skills involved in a complex task like vehicle control. For example, compensatory tracking is one of the component skills in many vehicle control tasks, and quite a lot is known about how to teach compensatory tracking. We know this because we can set up a cybernetic model against which the goings-on in the real laboratory or real life situation can be evaluated.

Thus when we look at training we are in the position of having a rapidly increasing body of knowledge in respect to sub-routines, sub-parts, sub-systems of control and are able to talk about optimality,

* See paper by E Stones (Ed.)

or at any rate "goodness" with respect to these entities. Thus, when we come to make a programme for teaching the whole skill or teaching the whole of a body of knowledge, then it seems to me that we can specify reasonable modules. The difficult question is whether putting together a lot of good modules yields a good whole. It is by no means obvious, incidentally, that it will do so. What we lack at the moment is a total theory of education or of complete programming for training systems. However it is as good a hunch as any other that we should try to optimise our modules first of all and put them together on the assumption that the composite programme will be effective. In that area of endeavour I think we can get quite a long way.

II CYBERNETIC METHODS OF INFORMATIONAL ANALYSIS

Now, with this preliminary admission of the limitations of the field, I would like to take for the first instance of the use of a cybernetic method the field of task specification and goal specification. Here the cybernetic approach calls for an informational analysis of the task. Commonly, tasks are broken down into sub-tasks on a more or less "ad hoc" basis, or else in terms of ergonomics or else in terms of factual mechanical data. For example, we distinguish tasks according to the movements performed in a complex skill, or the energy loadings or the amount of work that has to be done. These are often very good and very useful classification methods. On the other hand there are other aspects of any such skill which are in a sense more cybernetic. Instead of saying for example that when I walk across a room I am moving my legs in a particular manner and that this moving of the legs entails the expenditure of a certain amount of effort, I can concentrate instead upon the degree of correlation which has to occur between the right leg and the left leg in order that I shall achieve the goal of walking. If we take the imaginary situation where we are teaching someone to walk, then we might say that a certain amount of correlation must exist between the motions of the legs, or between variables indexing the motions of the legs. This is quite an abstract notion because the same comments would apply to a walking robot or to a walking physiological contraption like myself. So if I made a walker "in the metal", so to speak, the same comments would apply to the ultimate requirements of its walking that would apply to my walking.

An informational analysis is concerned with the amounts of correlation that must exist between variables (or sets of states) of a given entity or system, and it is relatively unaffected by the nature of what these states are; whether they happen to be states of legs or of the movements of legs or states of springs and pieces of metal.

By the same token one can extend the idea, as we are doing at the moment in my own laboratory, (for example), to clerical operations,

48

where, instead of my leg selecting one of several positions and my other leg selecting one of several other positions, some clerical worker has to select, say, one of N documents and in order to perform the task adequately has to perform one of M computations on one of these N documents. In this sense I can describe a clerical task in informational terms and I can specify "a priori" how much information must be transmitted between one selection and the other selection in order that the task can be carried out at all. Equally, of course, this type of analysis can be applied to, say, keyboard skills or to control skills. So, in a sense the informational branch of cybernetics, (informational analysis, which is a technique within cybernetics) allows us to state in the common currency of "information" that which has to be achieved in order to perform a certain sort of task. Hence it allows us to make an abstract but nevertheless interpretable specification of what should be done and to specify a goal in a new and, I think, valuable sense.

Likewise we can talk about such issues as information load which are closely related but not identical with "the amount of information that must be transmitted in order that a task should be done". Here I would like to take another example to indicate that "information load" is another essentially cybernetic method of measurement. If, for example, we take a task like morse transmission, or like teleprinter or typewriter operation, it used to be customary to talk about error on the one hand and rate of operation on the other. One got into grave difficulties in trying to measure what was going on because there is no common medium for measurement of error and rate. Now a cybernetic approach is to make a diagram (figure 1)

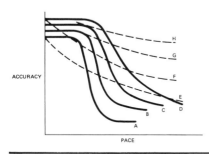

Figure 1. This diagram shows how accuracy is traded off against rate, so that the one is balanced against the other at a break-even point.

which represents accuracy as a function of rate and shows how accuracy is traded off against rate, so that the one is balanced against the other at a break-even point. For a novice one would get a curve similar to D. As we force the man to perform faster, his accuracy goes down. For a fully proficient subject the curve will perhaps be something like B. In other words we can force the rate up a great deal until we get to a limit at which it becomes necessary for the man to drop his accuracy. This, at least, is true for certain subjects, those with a "chemical" capacity in the sense of communication theory as in curves A, B, C, D. Some subjects do not have a chemical capacity. Their mistakes increase more or less continually with increasing rate as in curves E, F, G, H. We shall not consider these subjects for the idea of information capacity is inapplicable to them. In the extremes there is a family of curves A, B, C, D, as shown, and for any stage in training one can put a curve on such a diagram. Now, what a curve like this is saying is that there is a limited amount of transmission, in the sense of accurate replication of the input symbols into the output symbols which is characteristic of a man at a certain stage in performance. We are considering a man as an information system where an input is provided (in the case of morse transmission this input would consist in symbols to be transcribed) and an output is received (the written message or the output of the morse key). The man, regarded as an information transmitting channel, can transmit just the number of symbols per second indicated by the inflexion point. The accuracy - rate curves are simply a way of practicalising the notion of information transfer. So here is a typical cybernetic measuring technique. Further it is possible to extrapolate from the accuracy rate curves obtained at a series of forced rates in order to obtain a subject's rate at a given accuracy, say at around 95% accuracy. This yields a single figure (rate at a given accuracy).

   This sort of measurement has been used in connection with morse by the Army operational research unit and in connection with tele-printing by ourselves, and it appears to be quite a successful type of measuring device which is also of predictive value. It can pre-sumably be used in connection with a vast number of other skills as well, and there is a deal of information in the literature about the signal/noise characteristics of man which bears upon just this topic.

III SUBJECTIVE UNCERTAINTY

This of course is not the only kind of measurement which can be made of performance in the cybernetic sense. It is particularly important here to notice that when we are dealing with man, we are always dealing with at least two senses of a word like "information". When I talk about information in the sense in which I was just talking about it, in other words as a measure of correlation between variates, which describes performance, I am talking about information from the point of view of an outside observer, the training officer perhaps. I am not talking about information from the point of view of the student. From the point of view of the training officer, information is calculated by determining the uncertainty of what will happen, given that something else happens, and this is the observer's or the teacher's uncertainty. It is an uncertainty specified over a set of alternatives like leg positions or selections of documents which the teacher says are relevant to the question in hand. But it is perfectly clear also that a student has his own uncertainties with respect to a skill. In aggregate these will represent what he calls the difficulty of the skill. These uncertainties may also be converted into information measures and if we talk in this way we are talking of course about subjective information measures or subjective uncertainties. Now it is possible to obtain measurements of the subjective uncertainty (and also the subject information content) of tasks in respect to the individual student. These measures can be extraordinarily useful and I think are going to come into fashion very much in the next few years.

The technique is as follows. Suppose a student is answering a multiple-choice questionnaire and that he has in all N questions to answer. Each question offers a number of alternatives. On dealing with a particular question in the questionnaire he chooses between, say, five alternatives. In the conventional situation he will be asked to make just one response, i.e. to choose one alternative out of the five, the one he believes to be correct. In using a measuring technique keyed to subjective uncertainty, we say to the man "well, if you feel absolutely certain about it, make one choice, which means that you have bet 100% on that and zero percent on the others. But you are not forced to do that. You may in fact have a genuine uncertainty at this point, and if so you can express this by presenting us with a number for each of the alternatives chosen so that the numbers add up to 100%".

We can therefore obtain a subjective measure of how the man would bet on these alternatives. This can be tied to scoring schemes in the sense that we can clearly score this questionnaire or test by weighting the number that he has assigned to a particular response in an appropriate manner.

If we do so straightforwardly there is a grave difficulty that the student can, as it were, cheat. He will gain more, in the sense that his mathematical expectation of the score will be greater if he opts for something which has the largest likelihood of being right and sets this alternative at 100%. If he did that, we would fail to get the information we are seeking, namely information about his distribution of uncertainty over the alternatives. In order to avoid this pathology Shuford and his colleagues have devised a number of interesting scoring schemes which inhibit the tendency to opt for a certainty. These scoring schemes assign scores or weights to the answers elicited in such a manner that the student's mathematical expectation of score taken over the whole test is maximised if, and only if, he produces numbers that are veridicial estimates of what he really thinks. The Shuford scoring systems may either be instrumented by paper and pencil methods or more conveniently they can be embodied

in a piece of special purpose equipment which guarantees that the
numbers do all add up to 100%, that the process of estimation is
rapid and that the student can easily see what he is doing within the
Shuford framework.

So here is another measuring technique which stems from cybernetics.
It is a measuring technique concerned with subjective uncertainty.
Clearly subjective uncertainty, just like objective uncertainty can be
used as an input to guide a tutorial process, just as well as it can
be used as an adjunct to a questionnaire or test. In the context of
teaching and training I have used these methods in connection with
code-learning skills, both to estimate people's uncertainty about what
they should do next, and to estimate their uncertainty as to what plan
of action they should adopt. I think these methods are going to become
very commonplace, as I mentioned earlier.

IV CONVERSATIONAL TEACHING SYSTEMS

The next point that I would like to go into concerns learning theory.
When we talk about teaching we are always talking of imposing some
method of taking the total educational goal and breaking it down into
educational sub-goals; in other words taking the whole plan and breaking it down into modules of instruction which are addressed to
achieving sub-goals of the total goal. It is very nice to think that we
have so much omniscience that we can perform this exercise success-
fully and to some extent this numinous pose is empirically supported.
There is ample evidence to suggest that providing a plan of instruction
(as we do when designing a teaching programme) is better than
allowing the student to muddle along on his own. The fact is that
when left on his own the student tends to get into a mess for all sorts
of reasons. He has got to find his way through a cognitive maze and
break down the task into sub-problems which are small enough to be
learned about. So whatever kind of plan we produce, provided it be
moderately logical, is likely to be better than just muddling through.
Nevertheless we are not as almighty with respect to the prescription
of plans as we often like to think we are. In fact, the student comes
to the task in which he is going to be trained with a predisposition to
adopt plans of his own. He has, as it were, embedded in him an
internal teaching machine (we often refer to it as the attention
directing mechanism) and he uses as the grist to its mill a collection
of learning strategies which are of the student's own invention. These
he tries to employ. When we are stipulating a teaching strategy,
when we are acting as a teacher, then in a certain sense we are
usurping the right of the student to choose his own way of going about
things. Now we did say that it was usually better to choose a well
defined teaching plan than to allow the student to muddle ahead by
"free learning" using whatever rather hazy strategies he has got, but

an interesting conclusion which has come about through cybernetic research is as follows.

It is far better to engage the student in a sort of conversation about how he ought to learn. I have already ranked free learning as worse than an organised strategy (than programming if you like), and I am now saying that even better than programming is the sort of conversational interaction in which the student is presented with strategic alternatives and is allowed to choose between them (after being presented with some advice to begin with). Of course he can invent a few novel strategies of his own if he likes, which are added to the list of possibilities. During the conversational process he is guided by information culled from his performance which reveals features of his competence with respect to the task of which the student himself is frequently unaware. For example we may make an examination while he is performing the task of his subjective uncertainties, an estimation of his latencies in performance, etc. In general the competence data will represent features of competence such as memory capacity, levels of confidence etc., which, as I mentioned, the student is not directly aware of. So we now engage him in conversation in respect to a strategy of performance and in respect to the choice of a strategy of performance. Roughly speaking, we do as follows: so far as possible we allow a student liberty in choosing how he should learn, having once indicated to him the goals, the objectives of the learning process. We prohibit him from exercising this licence in so far as there is a manifest mis-match between his competence and the strategy which he has chosen to adopt. For example, some strategies rely upon the notion of learning from wholes to larger wholes. In contrast other strategies are concerned with a problem-solving, algorithmic orientation which some students have and others do not have. Now one can estimate whether a student is good at a heuristic approach or whether he is good at these sequential, algorithmic approaches.

We allow the student to choose his strategy, but if he chooses a strategy which is clearly unsuited to his competence, then we point this out to him and suggest (in fact we insist) that he chooses some other alternative strategy of learning.

The results of using this teaching method are quite dramatic. We have compared conversational teaching which entails discussion about strategies, with feedback - controlled teaching and with free learning in laboratory circumstances for quite complex and quite a number of coding and rule-application skills, and it turns out that the conversational approach wins dramatically, each time. I think this is quite in the spirit of liberal education and it is quite interesting to find that cybernetic experiments in the laboratory bear out what is perhaps the obvious to a humanistically inclined instructor.

V   METHODS OF CONTROL

The next topic is the actual manipulation of learning processes upon which I have already touched. Cybernetics takes a point of view in respect to procedures with which you are already familiar. Its point of view is this: as a teacher or trainer, you intend to exercise control over a learning process. In a certain sense you are in a position somewhat analogous to a control engineer, who has a process to control. As a result of this dogma, you must have a model of the process that you propose to control before you can attempt to control it. In this case it means that you must have some sort of model of how you believe that a student learns. Clearly this model might be of various sorts. Mathematical models are highly recommended but are usually too picayune in their conception to allow them to be applied to any but the most trivial learning situations. This is not just a quirk of mathematicians but simply that the necessary mathematical techniques are not yet fully developed. Again there are structural models and organisational models which have a mathematical flavour, in the sense that for example they can be computer programmed or represented by flow charts, but which are not fully quantifiable and there are those sorts of intuitive model which exist in the minds of good teachers and which are frequently not verbalised. The teacher or instructor has a model (he must have to be a good teacher). But frequently he cannot verbalise what it is, and the best way he can be brought to verbalise it is by asking him to look at some sort of training schedule and say "well I don't agree with that, because I know ...". This is the first point which comes out when we consider teaching as analogous to the control of learning. We have to have a model.

Now the next point is that our control operations might very well be divided into different sorts, and curiously enough these span the gamut of teaching techniques with which we are already familiar.

First of all, feed-forward control. This is ideally exemplified by the "Sight and Sound" method of typewriter instruction. The student is presented with a number of auditory stimuli representing symbols to be typewritten. At the same moment he is presented with cueing information in a large display – the replica of the keyboard, indicating what he should do, and the presentation goes on at a pre-determined rate for a time that is on the whole calculated to be good for the student. This entails of course a model, explicit or otherwise about how students learn, and of how they are supposed to combine the cueing information with the auditory stimulus in order to acquire the skill of typewriting. The method is feed-forward because nobody actually goes round to find out how the student is getting on and adjusts the display correspondingly. Indeed as this is a classroom display, not an individual display such an adjustment could only be carried out for the whole class. This sort of feed-forward teaching method should not be denigrated. It is often very valuable. It can be most effective and it tends to be extremely inexpensive.

Next there is the feed-back training method. A feed-back training method is one in which we adjoin to the original training schedule a modicum of knowledge of results, so that the student is given corrections, but more importantly we adjoin some operation which is carried out by the training device itself. The training device takes information from the student and uses it to adjust what is next presented. For example we might have a typewriting routine which presents knowledge of results to the individual student regarding his last key depression and then stops the tape which generates the characters which he is supposed to be typing until such time that he has got that one right. This is a very simple feed-back operation. Of course it can be elaborated, for example by using the information in the student's response sequence to modify the speed or sequence of characters to be presented. So a feed-back control device is not only one in which knowledge of results is given to the student so that he can correct his misconceptions, but also it is a system in which the machine itself, or the programme, responds in some appropriate way to the student.

Next there is adaptively controlled instruction. This is a fancy kind of feedback instruction typified by systems like the SAKI machine for keyboard instruction. In the paradigm case an adaptive machine makes selections from a source of problems which are posed to the student and which in their undiluted form would be unsolveable by the student. These problems are then passed through a box which in some sense simplifies the problems (and notice that in order to talk about simplification we clearly have to have a model, because "simplification" is "partial solution of a problem".) The student then responds. His response is compared with what he ought to have done in a comparator. A measure is obtained from this comparator, as a result of which a proficiency index is obtained. The proficiency measure goes into a decision rule and the decision rule is used to determine the degree of simplification. In a typical adaptive system the degree of simplification is reduced and the difficulty of the task is increased as the student learns to deal with the skill. Notice incidentally that this can be interpreted as keeping the student balanced on one of the curves shown in diagram 1. One would generally adjust the parameters of this system (the amount of increase in difficulty per increment of proficiency) in such a way that the student's perform-ance is balanced at a point on those curves which is optimal for learning. It turns out, surprisingly enough, that for many skills this point impells the student to perform with a remarkably small degree of accuracy. It is an interesting comment on learning as a whole that people tend to learn best when, if they do receive feed-back correction, they are still in the position of having to make quite a number of mistakes. They learn most efficiently when they are almost, though not quite overloaded.

Typical examples of adaptive systems are the compensatory tracking tasks such as Brian Gaines, Hudson and myself have studied. Consider a man doing compensatory tracking. He controls a simulated vehicle, the locus of which is represented by the position of a spot on a cathode ray tube. The vehicle is perturbed by a random noise signal and he has to compensate for the disturbance. In this case the problem's source consists of the random noise signal, the simplification is a variation in the mean amplitude of the random noise injected into the system. As the student becomes proficient so the amplitude of the random noise is increased. Likewise one can operate on the vehicle characteristics to make them more tricky to deal with.

Now finally of course there are conversational systems which may either be instrumented by instructors or instrumented by machines. These are systems where the subject has a level of discourse above this lower level discourse entailed by problem posing and problem solving.

At the higher level the student interacts with the teaching system in terms of preferred learning strategies. I have already pointed out that conversational systems are much better than feedback or adaptive systems for a certain number of tasks.

The following points bear upon the whole field of training. First of all a training method should be selected according to the learning model available. Only in the context of a model is it reasonable to prescribe one or other of these types of control. Next I would like to bring these into line with some of the notions of programmed learning. Clearly a linear programme is a feed-forward system with the sole exception that it gives knowledge of results to the student. But it responds in no way to what the student does. A branching programme is clearly a feed-back device in the terms that we have been discussing. Likewise a mathetics programme is of the feedback sort (here a rather elaborate model is used in which for example we say how the student will direct his attention across the page). Adaptive systems have been used chiefly in computer assisted instruction, but I would like to point out that the very elegant structural communication or systematics programmes of Bennett and Hodgson are adaptive in their conception and when mechanised effectively will be adaptive. When slightly developed some such systems may have some claim to the conversational mode as well, and I think that developments along these lines are particularly important.

Finally, although I have been talking mainly about bits of machinery, all of this can be translated into terms of programming or suggestions to teachers. Machinery is used as a matter of convenience. It is by no means mandatory unless of course there are physical or other limitations on the speed with which the teacher can pick up and react to information about the student.

To conclude therefore I would like to point out that these notions of cybernetics, although they are mechanistic in concept, by no means exclude the human being. Indeed they include the human being very strongly. For example, in a large tutorial system there will be at least two places where the human being comes into his own even if the system in question is maximally mechanised. One of these places will be when he is called for by the system to come and carry out some kind of tutorial or diagnostic task, and this is equally apposite in the classroom of an academic institution or in the workshop. Secondly quite a lot of the machinery can be economically replaced by a human being who carries out the specified procedures. Finally, and of paramount importance, humans are very often much more flexible than machinery. This is especially so if we are dealing with those complex formats at the outset - with long programmes consisting of a number of modules, or with an educational system in all its complexity, rather than one educational sub-routine.

The Selection and Use of Teaching Aids
A.J.Romiszowski

Contents

The aim of this book is not to provide a buyer's guide, or to demonstrate the versatility of particular items of equipment, but to present the reader with plausible teaching situations which may call for the use of certain equipment. The reader will then be able to apply the principles outlined to each problem posed, and to select appropriate presentation media.

Price 18 shillings

 Kogan Page
16 Grays Inn Road, London WC1

A systems approach to course planning at the Open University

by Dr. M. W. Neil, Instructional Systems Associates and Consultant, Open University

This paper is concerned with a brief and preliminary report of some of the work carried out by Mr. Macdonald-Ross, Mr. Alan Tout and myself in a series of special projects for the Vice-Chancellor of the Open University.

The approach adopted was derived in part from that which we produced as an addendum for the report of the Systems Approach Working Party of the First International Conference of Programmed Learning and Educational Technology at Goldsmith's College, London in April of this year (1969). A diagram outlining this approach was made available for members of the Working Party. (Figure 1)

It is, I believe, extremely important to distinguish between a 'systematic' and a 'systems' approach. The diagram referred to above is largely a 'systematic' approach with only hints of a 'systems' approach, interpreted as one which uses the concepts of cybernetics and general systems theory as bases for systems design. In practice, from hard experience, when it is required to convince those who are not familiar with systems ideas, it is best to proceed with a systematic approach first, using a minimum of technical jargon, and only at later stages to more sophisticated ideas which may present very real problems in communication.

We start, naturally enough, at much the same point as has already been introduced by the speakers from the Royal Navy. We ask 'what system and why are we concerned with it?' In the present instance no 'system' existed. The Open University challenge is that of creating a new system. Consequently, we first built a simple model of the University's main functional activity areas (figure 2). From this model we derived a primary functional activity in more detail which represented the essential processes for creating, preparing, producing and disseminating materials for students. Associated with this activity are a series of support activities and, of course, other activities introduced to ensure feed back from students (figure 3).

Our particular concern with the creation of the Open University system lay in the use which could be made of educational technology to guide and facilitate the primary functional activity mentioned above.

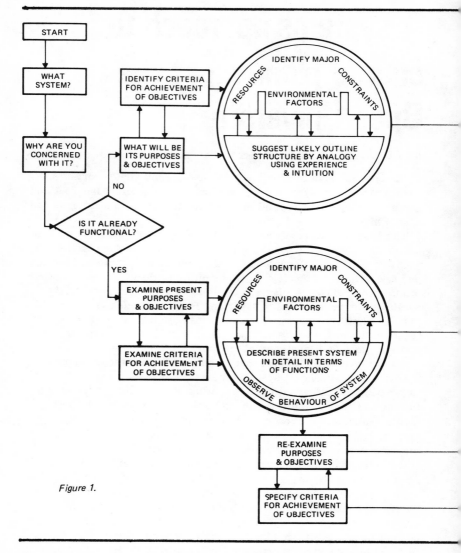

START

WHAT SYSTEM?

WHY ARE YOU CONCERNED WITH IT?

IDENTIFY CRITERIA FOR ACHIEVEMENT OF OBJECTIVES

WHAT WILL BE ITS PURPOSES & OBJECTIVES

IDENTIFY MAJOR
RESOURCES   CONSTRAINTS
ENVIRONMENTAL FACTORS

SUGGEST LIKELY OUTLINE STRUCTURE BY ANALOGY USING EXPERIENCE & INTUITION

NO

IS IT ALREADY FUNCTIONAL?

YES

EXAMINE PRESENT PURPOSES & OBJECTIVES

EXAMINE CRITERIA FOR ACHIEVEMENT OF OBJECTIVES

IDENTIFY MAJOR
RESOURCES   CONSTRAINTS
ENVIRONMENTAL FACTORS

DESCRIBE PRESENT SYSTEM IN DETAIL IN TERMS OF FUNCTIONS

OBSERVE BEHAVIOUR OF SYSTEM

RE-EXAMINE PURPOSES & OBJECTIVES

SPECIFY CRITERIA FOR ACHIEVEMENT OF OBJECTIVES

Figure 1.

It was therefore necessary to study the processes involved with a view to creating a satisfactory organisational structure to carry them out. The first step was to recognise, from the processes involved in the primary functional activity, likely boundaries for the sub-systems which would have to be set up. Boundaries are usually defined by discontinuities between processes – discontinuities in time, technology and space. A boundary implies a need for liaison and control between the sub-systems on either side. Further, a boundary

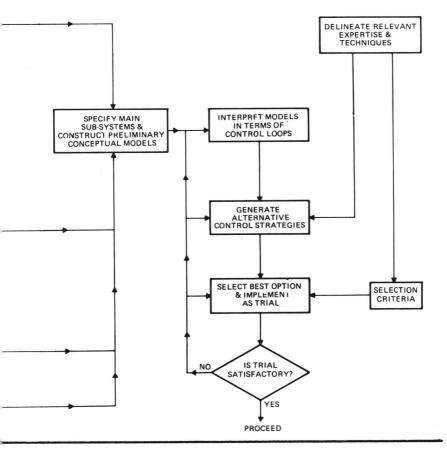

which may be made a factor in deciding upon organisational structure, needs to be considered not only in terms of the physical processes which it would separate but also in terms of the human groupings to which it would lead. Careful study of the primary functional activity model (figure 3), together with its implications for staffing, led us to identify four main sub-systems - the course team, a design sub-system, a television and radio technical sub-system and a 'business activities' sub-system. The last comprised production and market-

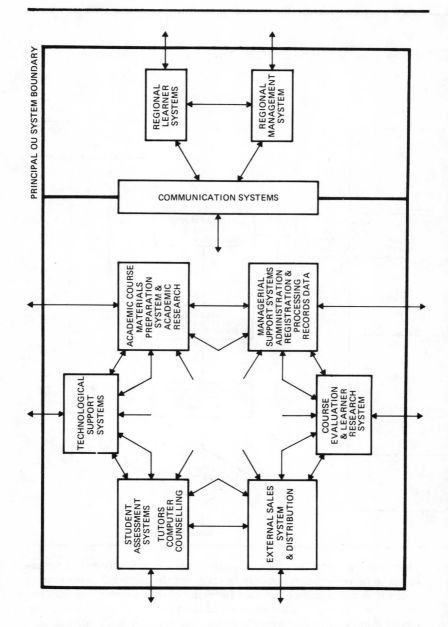

Figure 2. GENERAL INTERACTION MODEL — Open University major subsystems (first order resolution).

ing. Marketing was conceived as the operations required to package and store materials, and to distribute them to students, tutors and local study centres (since, in the Open University, the students will not come to the University, the University will go to the students, tutors and other staff all over the country using a variety of ways and means), and to sell University materials to institutional customers.

These functional sub-systems formed a basis for proposing alternative organisational structures which would be appropriate to carry out the primary functional activity processes.

A further crucial step is to indicate control mechanisms likely to be effective in regulating the overall system and in co-ordinating its sub-systemic parts. An important point in this connection is that if adaptation, feedback, evolution, self-regulation and so on, in the senses used by Professor George earlier, are to be achieved in practice, to however limited an extent, then the appropriate control mechanisms must arise from a sub-system superordinate to those sub-systems for which the mechanism has been devised. Such a superordinate system for control is often referred to as a 'meta-system'. Central to the idea of control are, of course, the nature, timing and amounts of information flowing within the total system, and the ways in which this information can be used.

Our terms of reference were mainly concerned with the roles of course teams and of the educational technology in supporting the course teams, and with the Vice-Chencellor's control and monitoring system. However, in attempting to adopt a total systems approach especially with regard to control mechanisms, it was necessary to scan areas other than those representing the focal points of our terms of reference. In our present state of limited knowledge about the applications of general systems theory in practice, a total systems approach is always a severe compromise between the desirables, the acceptables and the practicables. A further severe limitation on what can be done in practice arises from the commonly observed inability of the systems expert to communicate effectively with decision makers who are not familiar with concepts about systems. Our approach, especially with regard to control, was therefore one of extreme caution.

The process of designing a new system, using a systems approach, is not linearly sequential, but iterative and evolutionary. There is a main sequence of operations through which one goes - activities defined by a systems approach. One outlines a functional model, recognises primary functional activities, defines sub-systemic boundaries and so on. As one advances it becomes possible to improve the functional model and specify more clearly primary functional activities. Initial boundaries are modified or re-drawn. The whole process can be envisaged as a spiral arrangement of main activities with highly interactive and iterative linkages between points

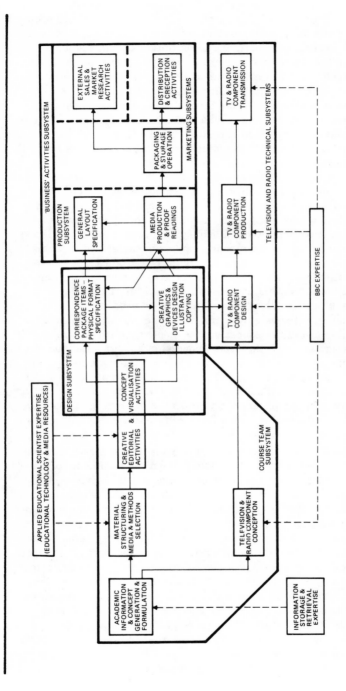

Figure 3. COURSE MATERIALS PREPARATION, PRODUCTION AND DISTRIBUTION – Preliminary functional model (second order resolution)

on the coil. In order to get started on a system design, there must be a preliminary specification of primary purposes and objectives. In the case of the Open University it was possible to derive these from the Planning Committees Report, the Vice-Chancellor and from the few members of staff in post at the time. At the same time, working parties were set up to provide much more detailed examinations of the University's educational concerns and practical procedures. Therefore, whilst working towards the achievement of preliminary objectives it becomes possible to continually refine and extend them and to assess how good we are at achieving them and to learn from our experience.

The procedures briefly outlined above, led us to select from possible organisational alternatives one proposing the formation of a strong educational technology unit, for which we used the name Applied Educational Sciences, which would be linked with the course teams and the design sub-system in clearly specified ways. We conceived of this unit as one which would evolve during the formative years of the Open University from one primarily serving the practical needs of the course teams to one primarily devoted to pure and developmental research and to developing post-graduate courses in conjunction with the future faculty of education. We worked out in detail how this unit might operate and made proposals for its development in practice. This part of our work is now practically complete, and staff have now been recruited to form the nucleus for the educational technology capability at the University. I should now like to discuss the course teams, and the way they work, in a little more detail.

There are four main faculties in the Open University at the moment. They are mathematics, science, social science and humanities. Each of these is responsible for the creation of a one year foundation course (four course in all) to start in January 1971. Each of the faculties has, at present, about eight members of staff. The amount of work required, if the result in the time available is to be anything like a learning system, is nothing short of heroic. Each faculty nominates a course team – at the moment, because there are so few of them, all members of faculty constitute the course team. The foundation course team designs and monitors the production of the materials. After a given stage, (discussed below) the course teams break up into working groups, each of which is required to produce the materials for a series of 'course units', of which there are about 36 in the foundation year for each course.

We produced initially a "first degree of resolution" model of the course team activities and then elaborated this into a whole network, which has four main phases, and about sixty activities. It must be emphasised that this network is experimental in the sense that, although each of the faculties will sooner or later have to carry out most of the activities specified, it is highly likely that they will wish

to work in different ways in practice. One of the fascinating pro-
spects for the educational technologists is to observe and learn from,
as well as to participate in, the different approaches adopted by
different faculties to the problem of producing high quality course
materials. In our experimental network there is a preliminary
phase during which the course team as a whole meets for several
weeks to determine the syllabus and curriculum. This is a very
detailed operation and establishes a frame work for all subsequent
stages. It is worth mentioning in passing that it is our present
recommendation that students should have a complete model of the
course - that is to say an inter-related diagram of the parts of the
course, a commentary on how it is put together and a detailed
synopsis of the content and the objectives (in behavioural terms)
which they are expected to meet. The Open University students will
rarely meet a tutor. They will be working largely on their own. We
believe therefore that half the battle towards their learning effectively
is that they should understand what it is that they are trying to learn
and why right from the start.

When the curriculum, scheduling, networking and so on are agreed,
the course team divides into working groups and these go through
three phases of operation (in our prototype experimental process).
In the first phase they specify in detail curricular items and objectives
in behavioural terms for a given course unit. We emphasise the
essentially reciprocal relationship between objectives and methods
of assessment, and objectives and methods of presentation. Therefore, having spelled out objectives, it is possible also in the first
phase to make first specifications for methods of assessment for the
correspondence materials and their methods of presentation, and
for television and radio material. These proposals are then submitted to the course team who may require certain modifications to
be made. The working group can then proceed to phase two, in
which the preparation of most of the materials occurs. During
this phase much informal consultation occurs between different
working groups. The materials are then submitted to the course
team, which comments and again may require some modifications.

In the final phase, studio operations are undertaken (initially by
the BBC) to produce the radio and TV components and "mock-ups"
of the correspondence materials are produced for the academics to
look at. These mock-ups provide material for developmental testing
to be carried out by the Applied Educational Sciences unit, which
will certainly lead to further modifications. Of course, full scale
validation tests on the materials will be performed once they are
issued to students, but it is essential that some form of developmental testing is carried out before materials actually go out. At
the conclusion of the third phase a final draft is produced and the
complete unit is submitted to the course teams and full scale production of materials occurs.

The scheduling of all this, and the design of its control system, present quite a problem. The members of a working group must work on more than one unit at a time if proper scrutiny of progress is to be made at course team level. The Dean of Faculty and the course team represent the first level of control. The schedule of work on all units for a foundation course is notified to the Vice-Chancellor whose office is responsible for monitoring work on all courses in all faculties and for co-ordinating this work with that of design and production. Periodic reports are made to the Vice-Chancellor's Office by course teams on progress at critical points (e.g. the completion of a phase) for each unit. The Vice-Chancellor takes action usually only 'by exception' - that is when scheduled dates are missed or when the work load on design or production looks like exceeding capacity, for example. Work on post-foundation courses for which the faculties will approximately double their staff in 1970, is due to start before the first units of the foundation courses go out to students. The time available for work on units is therefore severely limited, and the logistic problems are considerable.

We are indeed trying to make the Vice-Chancellor's Office into a true meta-control system and not just a mechanistic recording outfit. We hope, in fact, to introduce a little cybernetics and general systems theory into the design of the way that the Vice-Chancellor's Office operates as a control system, but this will undoubtedly take a long while and represent an evolutionary feature.

Systematic restructuring of teacher education

by E. Stones, University of Birmingham

I would like to stress that this is very much an interim report. We are still at the projection stage in this field of the analysis and planning of teacher education. Perhaps I ought to make quite clear what this field involves. Almost every university in the country has an area training organisation which embraces colleges of education in the area. Birmingham is one of the largest of these area training organisations with 18 colleges and about 9000 students. They all use the University School of Education as a focal centre for their meetings, for administration, services to teachers etc. Students at the colleges of education take either three year or four year courses, the latter leading to a B.Ed. degree. The University proper is mainly concerned with teaching students on advanced courses - teachers who have come back after some years in the field to do further studies - and students who have just graduated who are taking a one year course in education.

The research project with which I am presently engaged was not initiated as a direct application of a systems approach. In fact I suspect that if I used this term many of the people involved would not quite know what I meant. But the problem was this: all sorts of developments are taking place in education and training. In some instances industry and the forces have taken major steps here. Sometimes people in other aspects of education have not taken the same interest. If one examines what goes on in many colleges and departments of education one will probably find that they are operating the same kind of teaching system as they have been operating for many years. In a recent survey we found that the predominant teaching method employed in our area in the colleges of education is the straightforward lecture. One of the problems has been the tremendous expansion in the colleges so that they have not had the time to assimilate new ideas or to change their methods of teaching into line with some current ideas of the type being discussed at this conference.

We therefore have this conflict between what we are operating and what some of us feel we ought to be operating. Some of us wished to examine this problem because even the students could see this conflict. We tell them one thing - new developments, Nuffield maths,

Nuffield Science etc. – but very often the practice in the colleges does not keep pace with these developments.

In addition, and perhaps more importantly, we wished to set up psychological experiments aimed to investigate processes involved in human learning and instruction.

Within the area training organisation we have a "Colleges of Education Research Group" and this embraces people from all the colleges in the area who are interested. We have about 150 college turors who are interested or actively involved in working parties on the project. The University Department operates as a servicing centre, but does not direct activity. Nobody at the University can say: "You will apply a systems approach". Changes are brought about by discussion and the presentation of information.

One rather difficult problem in this area is the specification of precise objectives prior to teaching. The analysis of existing practices with a view to change is seen as a real threat by many teachers. Also when you start a systematic analysis of any sort, you presume that at the end of the day you will end up with some sort of prescription. Here again one meets resistance both emotional ... "are you going to tell me what to do? .... what to teach? .... which kind of projector to use?" and intellectual in that the experts do not always agree among themselves.

We are in this project investigating only one section of a college of education course ..... Education. In most colleges this at present comprises 5 distinct disciplines ... psychology, philosophy, curriculum studies, history and sociology, and for these 5 disciplines we have 5 working committees. We also have 3 "service" committees investigating systems analysis, evaluation and educational technology. These committees meet to investigate current practices with a view to their improvement and the application of more systematic methods to the teaching of the 5 subjects. We have in mind the joint production of materials and joint development of systematic methods of assessment of courses. Because we have this coverage of several disciplines we shall be able to replicate experiments in different fields and hope to achieve results of more general application.

We are not yet at the stage of having a fully worked out model of our approach. The systems analysis committee is hoping to produce such a model of the research project as a whole. They have so far produced a network for the organisation of school practice which is proving quite useful in several colleges.

The general strategy we have adopted however is a cyclical one. The first thing the committees considered was the objectives of the course. The best one can say at this stage is that these are approximate objectives. In particular we have to work within the general framework of existing practice, as we are not in a position to carry through major organisational changes. We could not start in this project with a clean slate, as perhaps one can in planning the Open University or other new projects. Our main aim in stating objectives was to optimise teaching procedures within the broad confines of the existing course structure.

When you consider the problem of the stating of objectives in behavioural terms as enunciated by Bloom, Mager and other experts, you find discrepancies in the terminology used. Bloom for example allows such terms as "Knowledge" whereas Mager does not. We have found Bloom's approach very useful in that a consensus of opinion is more easily reached. However, often this consensus is spurious and on closer analysis we find that different people mean different things by the same (stated) objective. We have found that a useful approach to overcome this difficulty is to consider the type of learning that is involved in mastery of the objective. Here we have found Gagné's model of the categories of learning most applicable.

In attempting to get agreement on objectives in the teaching of educational psychology, we consulted colleagues in the field and we carried out a survey of the colleges in the country. We have come to the conclusion that it is probably not possible to get complete consensus on objectives in this field at the moment. What we shall have to do is to define objectives in certain areas where most agreement can be reached, produce materials, try them out and refine our objectives as we go, a sort of cyclical, spiral approach. A further problem which recurred over the period taken to define objectives (about one year) was the difficulty that many practising college lecturers had with distinguishing between statements of objectives and statements of content

We are now at the stage in some of the committees of having reached some consensus of agreement on some of the objectives involved and are now proceeding to an analysis of the tasks involved. We are looking for the concepts and the principles involved. We also ask what kind of learning is going on in the various situations, how are we going to present stimuli, what are the appropriate stimuli, what is the nature of the feedback going to be, what kinds of examples are we going to present. In some areas we have proceeded beyond this point to a consideration of the materials we are going to use. We are trying to introduce a variety of media, programmes, textbooks, research papers, source documents, recorded discussions, tutorials, simulation methods, etc. Our approach is to produce modules of instruction, so that eventually we shall be able to present the student with considerable choice in his course. We also intend to give him more precise directions, perhaps in the form of a flow-chart of his course, and give him some element of responsibility for working his way through.

One problem with this approach is the storage and ready retrieval of instructional material. This is not difficult in the early stages, but as the system is more widely used, these problems will grow. There is a need here for further work on the design of efficient control systems to give students ready access to the materials and the facility of readily monitoring their progress.

With regard to evaluation, we are developing entry tests and terminal tests. We have already used some objective testing methods in this field. One college is experimenting with simulation techniques for evaluation. Some of us are trying to get away from the traditional 3-hour essay type examination, and are including other assessment techniques such as criticisms of research papers, analysis of teaching problems, the construction of short programmes or tests - in short a trend to actual practical situations rather than descriptive essays. Furthermore we do not go along with the principles of end-of-course assessment, but favour rather some form of continuous monitoring of progress, monitoring designed not only to assess the student but also, indeed mainly, to assess the course and to plan future modifications. Thus by applying many of the practical principles of programmed learning to a fairly broad, not too well defined field, we are hoping to produce an efficient, controllable teaching system. We shall in the end wind up with a dynamic, adaptable system, which I suppose one could refer to as a cybernetic system. However, the approaches we are using are not based on a very rigorous systems theory but are rather pragmatic. We are beginning to work in a more systematic manner, attempting to follow a model, but with such a large and varied group of people involved, such progress is necessarily slow.

The application of general systems theory to secondary education

by Peter Hodge, Jordanhill College of Education

I. SOME FUNDAMENTAL CONCEPTS OF GENERAL SYSTEMS THEORY

I.1 Definition of 'system' and 'systems approach'

The term 'system' has been variously defined by various writers, but perhaps we can initially accept the definition of Ackoff (1960) who suggests that a system is 'any entity, conceptual or physical, that consists of independent but interrelated parts'. As Beer (1959) and others point out, the selection of a particular system is always arbitrary and depends upon the interests of the person analyzing the whole and its constituent parts, and the relationships between them.

The 'systems approach' represents a set of procedures whereby thorough analysis of a system may be undertaken. Silvern (1968a) summarises these under four events which usually follow a set order: (a) analysis is performed on the existing system to identify the parts and the interrelationships; (b) synthesis is performed to combine these various elements together with new elements previously unrelated; (c) models are constructed to predict the effectiveness of the system; and (d) simulation is carried out prior to implementation of the system in real life.

I.2 Types of System: deterministic vs. probabilistic

Behavioural systems are complex probabilistic systems: that is, their behaviour can never be determined precisely as in the case of deterministic systems. Instead, the investigator is concerned with predicting the probable changes that will occur over a period of time, and such predictions will depend for their accuracy upon the information available at a given moment.

I.3. Types of System: open vs. closed

All behavioural systems are 'open' – that is, they import energy and/ or information from and export it back into their environment in the form of inputs to and outputs from the system. In education we may talk of 'open' and 'relatively closed' systems, since the systems with which we are concerned can never be totally closed (Katz & Kahn, 1966).

I.4 System and System Environment

One of the important relationships is that between the system under study and the system environment. The 'system environment' may be defined, in common with Hall & Fagen (1956), as 'the set of all objects, a change in whose attributes affects the behaviour of the system, and also of those objects whose attributes are changed by the behaviour of the system'.

McMillan & Gonzalez (1965) suggest that one way of distinguishing between system and environment is to consider whether or not an activity is subject to management control. Those factors or activities which are beyond the control of management can be classed as system environment. If a general theory of instruction is to be created, it would appear to be important to identify those factors that are outside management control.

I.5 Structure and Process

It is important to distinguish between 'structure' and 'process' in analyzing systems. Miller (1965) defines the structure of a system as 'the static arrangement of a system's parts at a moment in three-dimensional space'. On the other hand he defines process as 'the dynamic change in the matter-energy or information of a system over time'. Bertalanffy (1952) suggested that 'the antithesis between structure and function .... is based upon a static conception of the organism .... What are called structures are slow processes of long duration, functions are quick processes of short duration'.

The essential difference between structure and process, when various semantic difficulties have been removed, appears to be that between a static arrangement and the concept of continual dynamic change. This distinction is important when one is attempting to model a system.

I.6 Elements of Open Systems: Inputs, Process Components and Outputs

Open systems can be said to comprise three main elements: (a) inputs of energy and/or information, (b) process components (or 'through-puts'), and (c) outputs of energy and/or information (Miller, 1965; Coombs, 1968). Open systems frequently possess a fourth component – a control mechanism or comparator which acts as a regulator of system output.

I.7 Regulation in Open Systems: Feedback and Error Signal Generator

A comparator regulates a system by feeding back information and/or energy from its output back into its input. This usually involves an 'error signal generator' which monitors deviations from the desired output and generates a signal which leads to modification of system input. The relay of information back is termed feedback.

Feedback may be positive or negative (Bertalanffy, 1950; Beer, 1959; et al). When the deviation in output from the desired state is amplified, feedback is positive. When the deviation is reduced, negative feedback is used.

I.8 Adaptive Systems

Systems which adapt or adjust themselves to changes in their environment are termed 'adaptive' systems (Ashby 1956; Beer, 1959; Miller, 1965; et al). The work of Ashby and Pask (1961) in particular has been concerned with the way such adjustment takes place. The main component in such mechanisms is the use of complex feedback systems.

I.9 Equilibrium and Steady State: Homeostasis

'When opposing variables in a system are in balance, that system is in equilibrium with regard to them' (Miller, 1965). Miller goes on to distinguish between equilibrium, which is a static concept, and steady state which represents a dynamic balance between opposing variables within certain definable limits. The process of self-regulation by which a system preserves itself in a steady state is called 'homostasis' (Bertalanffy, 1950; Ashby 1956; Miller, 1965; et al).

The concepts of steady state, equilibrium and homeostasis spring from biological mechanisms of self-preservation in the face of a constantly changing, and sometimes hostile, environment. In the context of organizations, steady state represents the notion of maintaining the orderliness of the system in the face of energy or information stresses. Types of stress in living systems are outlined by Miller (1965).

I.10 Information, Entropy and Negative Entropy

The concept of entropy has been used to refer to the way in which the elements in physical systems tend to become more randomly dispersed over time. (This was first stated in the Second Law of Thermodynamics). Since then, however, entropy has been used in information theory to describe the statistical characteristics of information passing through a communications channel (Shannon & Weaver, 1949).

The application of such a concept in the context of open behavioural systems has been taken further by various investigators, including Prigogine (1955), Bertalanffy (1950), and Katz & Kahn (1966). The essential difference between the concept of entropy as applied to physical systems and the idea of 'negative entropy' as used in the context of behavioural systems lies in the discovery that while the entropy of physical systems tends to increase - that is, there is greater randomness of the elements over time – in the case of behavioural systems, the more complex the system becomes, the less random is the distribution of energy – that is, there is greater differentiation between the parts and structures.

I.11 Variety and Information: the Law of Requisite Variety
Variety is a term used to refer to the differences in energy and/or information with which a system has to cope. Such differences involve the concept of regulation and the way in which the degree of regulation achieved can be measured (Ashby, 1956). Since we are concerned with predicting the probability of different outcomes in complex behavioural systems, such quantification of the amount of variety in a system is an important prerequisite to being able to control the system.

The Law of Requisite Variety, which was first stated by Ashby (1956), is a measure of regulation. In its simplest form it states that the variety in the control system must be as great as the variety in the system or parts that are to be controlled. As Ashby puts it, 'only variety can destroy variety'.

I.12 Equifinality
Bertalanffy (1950) was one of the first to show that open systems display the characteristic of 'equifinality' – that is to say, the final (desired) state may be arrived at from a number of different initial states and by different routes. As open systems develop methods of self-regulation and control, the amount of equifinality may be reduced (Katz & Kahn, 1966).

II. ANALYZING THE TEACHING-LEARNING PROCESS AS A SYSTEM: INPUTS, PROCESS COMPONENTS AND OUTPUTS
II.1 Defining the System
Systems analysis is concerned with the analysis of a whole system and its parts with a view to identifying the relationships between the various components. As such systems analysis may consider macro-structures or micro-structures, or both, it is important, therefore, at the outset to define the system chosen for study.

The system chosen for study in this paper is the instructional system in secondary schools. As various writers have pointed out, all systems may ultimately be regarded as sub-systems of the universe (Beer, 1959; Pask, 1961). Silvern (1968b) and Hoyle (1969) indeed regard the educational process as a sub-system as opposed to a system in its own right. For the purpose of this analysis, however, it may be more convenient to regard the educational system as a whole as representing the system environment and to confine our attention mainly to that part of formal education represented by secondary schools.

It should be noted here that a distinction is drawn between formal and informal learning, formal learning or instruction being within the control of the school. That this distinction is necessary is shown by the number of psychological studies of learning where findings are related only to variables manipulated under controlled experimental conditions. It may also be useful to draw this distinction in the light of McMillan & Gonzalez' (1965) definition of system environment which was mentioned earlier, since those factors which are beyond the control of management in secondary schools may or may not be controllable by the educational system as a whole.

II.2 Defining the System Environment

In the context of the secondary school instructional system, it is necessary to examine both (a) the general and (b) the immediate environments of the system, since secondary schools may be regarded as a sub-system of the educational system as a whole.

If we look first at the general environment of the educational system, it would appear that there are three major related systems with which it interacts (Fig 1). These are - (1) the Social System,

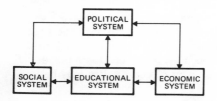

Figure 1. General system environment

(2) the Political System, and (3) the Economic System. If we wish to specify the relationships, we might add that the social system represents the needs, values, demands and priorities of society; the political system provides the structure for ordering these demands in terms of priorities and the machinery for implementing society's demands; and the economic system determines the extent to which men, money and materials are made available to satisfy demands. The relationships between the educational and social systems are described by Coombs (1968).

If we consider the immediate environment of the secondary school system itself, we can identify some of the major paths of information and energy flow between the various systems (Fig 2). These, it is suggested, include the flow of materials and information between the formal system in secondary schools and the non-formal educational or social system, as outlined by Coombs, the primary school, and the higher educational, vocational and adult education systems. What is important for our purpose here is to identify the systems which

He is strong, confident, dismissive, with — gesture
the world & its commonplaces. She is melting,
not being taken, but giving, what she alone can give,
Her woman's ingredients are
Her delicate graceful limbs exhibit bountiful   × manualiveness

So, with the inward eye, I see your warm
          pulsating

Life does not encompass the eternal

But change, inevitable change.

KOGAN PAGE LTD.
16 GRAYS INN ROAD LONDON WC1X 8BR   Tel: 01-242 8737

QTY.		DUE			D 006798 DELIVERY NOTE
1	Systems Approach To Education & Training (16)	£1.25	£1.25		
	POSTAGE		£0.15		
		£1.40			

Paid 1/6/71

DATE
14.5.71.

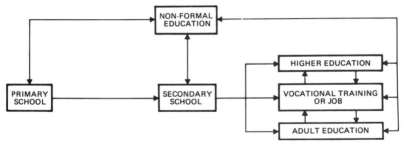

Figure 2. Immediate environment of Secondary School sub-system

are directly related to that of the secondary school in order to
identify the sources of inputs to, and the systems which receive the
outputs from the secondary school system.

Silvern (1968b), in an analysis of the information cycles in
occupational or vocational education, remarks that 'because the
secondary school is a subsystem and not a system ... the dynamicism
of this school is determined not by internal energy but by inputting
of energy from outside the school .... Changes in a specific
occupation in the real-life situation should be anticipated by the
school. Some occupations will tend to change more quickly than
others so the school will have to sensitize itself to those more
dynamically'. The need for constant examination of the changing
demands of society and related systems is also argued by Coombs.
The system must be adaptive if its outputs are to meet the changing
requirements of its environment.

II.3 Analyzing the System: Inputs, Process Components and Outputs
What are the inputs, process components and outputs of the secondary
school instructional system? Eraut (1969), for example, defined
a learning system as '(1) the resources, both human and material,
which enable students with one set of characteristics (the system's
input) to emerge with another set of characteristics (the system's
output); (2) the relationships between these resources; and (3) the
interactions between students and resources'. Unfortunately, he
does not define the resources to which he refers. (Compare this
statement with that of Neil (1969) who suggested that the three major
components are: (a) learners; (b) teachers; and (c) materials.)

Coombs (1968), in an analysis of international educational systems,
lists twelve major components of any educational system. These are:
(1) aims and priorities; (2) students; (3) management; (4) structure
& time schedule; (5) content; (6) teachers; (7) learning aids; (8)
physical facilities (for housing the process); (9) technology; (10)
quality controls; (11) research; and (12) costs. He is concerned

largely with the macro-structure of an educational system as a whole, and not with any particular sub-system, but his analysis may be a useful starting point for more detailed study of the problems within the secondary school.

The primary inputs, Coombs argues, are the students who also represent the system output. And here, it is perhaps important to distinguish between two uses of the term 'inputs'. Inputs may be either (a) the objects or persons processed by a system (to use a crude industrial analogy), or (b) the total input of men, materials, and information which enable the system to function. Unless otherwise stated, the term is used in this paper in the first sense. The inputs then are acted upon by the process components. These components can be analyzed in terms of (a) the elements (i.e. men, materials, and equipment) and (b) the functions of these elements (i.e. what each does). Outputs are represented by students whose characteristics as measured upon entry have, it is assumed, been altered in some way. The term 'output' itself involves the notion of 'standards of acceptability' or what Coombs calls 'quality controls'. In education these include the achievement of certain standards or criteria as measured by tests, examinations, ratings and so on, which are in turn based upon the various aims and objectives of the system. The standards of acceptability may be either (a) internal (i.e. established within the school itself) or (b) external (i.e. set by outside bodies or society as a whole).

II.4 Defining the Transformations from Input to Output: Problems of Definition

In order to define the changes from input to output, it is necessary first to define the input characteristics, the output characteristics and the system goals and objectives (or standards of acceptability). This assumes that (a) the characteristics are measurable, and (b) that the measures used are valid and reliable. It also assumes that the system objectives can be clearly identified, since one cannot adequately assess achievement of standards if the standards themselves are inadequately defined. The contribution of programmed learning in this area has been in showing the utility of short-term objectives as a means to defining broader, less definable long-term goals.

A further problem of definition exists when one comes to analyze the various stages within the secondary school system. At the practical level, it is evidently not enough to define initial input and final output; one must also identify and define the input and output criteria for each stage within the overall process if the 'couplings' between the stages are to be satisfactorily achieved. For example, the outputs of the second year must correspond with the input requirements for the third, and so on. This entails analysis of the hierarchies of learning tasks, as Gagné suggested.

II.5 Process Components: Relation between System & System Environment

Of the twelve components suggested by Coombs, four can be excluded from our description of process components. These are the students (who we have defined as the system inputs), and technology research and costs (which are included under other headings). It may be useful to examine briefly the relationships between the remaining components and the system environment.

AIMS – determined by the social and political systems, as well as by policy-making bodies within the educational system; usually stated in highly generalised form, they are represented by statements in syllabuses (see Content).

MANAGEMENT – structure, composition and organization of management is determined by outside educational bodies (e.g. Local authorities, statutory bodies, and governing bodies); composition of management is dependent upon man-power available and the economic system.

TEACHERS – external factors influencing teacher behaviour include: (a) own learning abilities; (b) home background and social environment; (c) training and experience; (d) motivation and aspirations; (e) qualified man-power available; (f) selection procedures and standards of appointing bodies; (g) number of teaching posts available.

CONTENT – dependent upon (a) the state of knowledge at any one time; (b) the composition of curricula; (c) the syllabuses drawn up by examining bodies; (d) the requirements of social, political and economic systems.

STRUCTURE & SCHEDULE – dependent upon (a) aims, (b) content, (c) management, (d) teachers, (e) physical facilities, (f) numbers of pupils; as such is determined partly by the regulations of outside bodies, and partly by management within the school.

MEASURING INSTRUMENTS – dependent upon (a) aims, (b) content, (c) examining bodies and curricular boards, (d) techniques available.

LEARNING AIDS – dependent on technological developments, and economic resources available.

PHYSICAL FACILITIES – dependent upon political and economic
        systems, and determined by local authorities and national
        bodies.
    This is intended to be nothing more than a brief, and extremely
superficial, outline of the kinds of relationships between system
components and aspects of the system environment. Much more
detailed analysis is required of the individual elements within these
eight major process components and the way in which these factors
are related to specific aspects of the environment which are within
the control of management at the educational, social or political level.

II.6 Analyzing Elements of System Components
The next stage in the analysis will include identification of the
elements within each of the eight major components already outlined,
including the analysis of the different patterns of management
structures to be found in the secondary school, the hierarchies of
learning tasks involved in syllabus statements (cf. Scottish Education
Department, Consultative Committee on the Curriculum, Curriculum
Paper No. 7 'Science for General Education, Edinburgh: HMSO,
1969), school organizational structure and timetabling schedules,
measuring instruments used in schools, learning aids, and physical
facilities. Such an analysis represents formidable problems, but
would appear to be a necessary prerequisite to system modelling
and simulation at a practical level.

III. APPLICATIONS OF GENERAL SYSTEMS THEORY TO THE
MODELLING OF THE SECONDARY SCHOOL INSTRUCTIONAL
SYSTEM
Before considering some of the possible applications of general
systems theory to the design of secondary school instructional
systems, it may be useful to summarise briefly the types of models
that are commonly used and the limitations of each type.

III.1 Types of Models: Functions and Limitations
Systems are frequently represented by models which, as Chorley
(1964) points out, are 'idealizations of a segment of the real world'.
There are three main kinds of models – (a) iconic (little more than
hypotheses, usually presented in graphical form); (b) analogue
(using physical equipment to produce an analogous process to the
real system); and (c) symbolic (usually 'pure' mathematized models
capable of quantification and verification). In addition to this, as
George (1969) remarks, models may be either static or dynamic.
    Models have several functions. These include –
(a) the projection of theories, laws, or hypotheses about the
     universe around us;

(b) the transmission of information in an economical and highly compressed form;

(c) the generation of fresh hypotheses, by oversimplifying the real world and thus highlighting areas where further research is needed.

There are, however, a number of dangers in using models as well as limitations of the models that we can use. These include –

(a) taking the model as being the 'real' system

(b) inferring too much from the kind of model used (e.g. using an iconic model as if it were capable of rigorous verification)

(c) oversimplifying the real system in the model

(d) overspecifying the real system in the model so as to be too exclusive

(e) attempting to quantify parameters in symbolic models when the parameters themselves may not be susceptible to the use of existing quantification techniques

(f) using a static model to represent a dynamic system

There is also the problem of the level of analysis (or resolution level as it is sometimes called) represented by the models used.

III.2 The 'Black Box' Approach to the Secondary School Instructional Process

One of the most useful concepts provided by general systems theory and cybernetics is the 'Black Box' approach, which has been introduced by cybernetics in particular to contain the problem of system complexity and uncertainty in highly complex probabilistic systems. It should be noted that such an approach is not particularly new in education: the behaviourist school of psychology has long used the S–O–R model as the basis for psychological investigations into the learning process. The utility of such a concept lies in the emphasis on the observable features of the system to be controlled rather than on the operational details which in our present state of knowledge are inadequately understood.

If we apply such a concept to our initial analysis of the components of the system in secondary schools, we may hypothesize a simplified model of the kind shown in Figure 3. As Ashby (1956) points out,

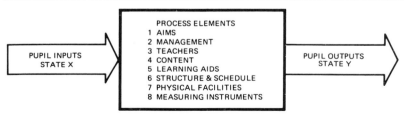

Figure 3. The secondary sub-system: 'BLACK BOX' approach (after COOMBS, P. 1968)

the primary data of any investigation of a Black Box consists of a
sequence of values represented by the vector (input state, output
state) over a period of time. It should be possible, in theory at
least, to describe the transformations within the various sub-systems
provided we can define the inputs and outputs and also the major
process components.

In order to quantify the input and output states, it is first necessary
to be able to identify the number of <u>distinguishable</u> input and output
characteristics, as well as the number of inputs and outputs. In this
sense, the variety of pupil inputs will be represented by (the number
of pupil inputs) x (the number of distinguishable characteristics
possible for each pupil). The problem is whether or not such
attempts to quantify the input variety are practicable or useful? In
the case of a Box with only eight inputs and one output, if each input
is capable of only two possible values, the number of possible input
states is 2^8. Even assuming that it were possible to define the
various possible input characteristics of each pupil, the number of
possible states for one pupil would be so vast that it is difficult to
see how such quantification would be useful with existing techniques.

III.3 A Generic Model of the Teaching-Learning Process as a System

It may be more useful to use the concept of the Black Box at the
iconic level without attempting to quantify the parameters initially.
This type of approach was suggested by the present author in the
model shown in Figure 4 (Hodge, 1967), which utilizes the input-
output technique. It was suggested that the instructional process
could be regarded as an open system of input-process-output, with a
closed-loop or cyclical sub-system which acts as a regulator of system
output. This regulator mechanism consists of measurement (in the

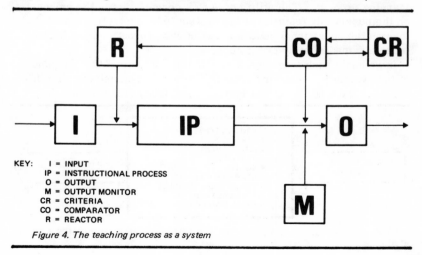

KEY: I = INPUT
        IP = INSTRUCTIONAL PROCESS
        O = OUTPUT
        M = OUTPUT MONITOR
        CR = CRITERIA
        CO = COMPARATOR
        R = REACTOR

Figure 4. The teaching process as a system

form of tests, examinations, etc), a set of criteria or objectives which define output standards, and a comparator device (either human or mechanical) which compares the results obtained from measurement with the 'ideal' criteria established by the school or examinations board. If a pupil satisfies the criteria, he may be classed as output (either to another stage in the system, or out of the system). If not, then, in theory at least, he should be referred to a remedial process after decisions have been taken as to the suitable remedial treatment by a reactor mechanism. The function of measurement in this sense is to enable regulation of system output to take place, along lines similar to those in engineering and cybernetic systems.

III.4 Cyclical Sub-Systems in Teaching
The same author in a later paper (Hodge, 1969) suggested that within the overall open system of the instructional process in schools are a number of cyclical sub-systems similar to that used to regulate the overall system. The evidence for the validity of this argument is to be found in the work of researchers in the field of computer-based systems such as Coulson & Silberman (1961), Stolurow (1965), and others, as well as in the field of adaptive mechanisms of the kind described by Pask (1961). It was argued that while there is evidence for supporting iconic models such as the one shown here, the use of analogue or symbolic models in this area is subject to the problems of quantification mentioned earlier, and that quantification as such is probably only possible in specific operations within a single subsystem. Smallwood (1962), for example, suggested that a case can be made for the use of decision theory in teaching providing the process is automated. The problem comes when the degree of control possible with automatic equipment is missing from the organization of the teaching-learning process in schools.

III.5 Feedback, Homeostasis and Steady State
The concept of cyclical sub-systems acting as regulators of output also involves the concepts of feedback, homeostasis and steady state outlined earlier. The system will be adaptive and in a steady state if it can utilise information about pupil input, progress during process, and output to generate an error signal that will lead to a modification of the organizational procedures in order to meet the demands of the various sub-systems within it and the related systems which it serves. This assumes the existence of instruments for obtaining information on pupils at all stages, and communications channels to ensure that decisions are taken on the basis of accurate information which can be rapidly obtained. And here, it would appear that a great deal more information is needed about the measuring instruments used in schools for diagnostic purposes and the channels of communication whereby information can be obtained.

III.6 Negative Entropy & Entropy

The concepts of negative entropy and entropy may also be useful in the school context. The latter would appear to have possible applications for the quantification of the amount of information to be encoded, processed and decoded by pupils during learning as well as the information required and the channels that exist for carrying out management decisions.

Negative entropy would appear to be relevant when considering the problems of management structure and school organization, in the sense that the larger the school, the greater the differentiation that will occur between the various departments leading to increased specialisation. This may conflict at times with present attempts to bring about a rapprochement between the various disciplines at the curricular level.

III.7 Variety

As mentioned earlier, the concept of variety would seem to be particularly relevant in the secondary school in the sense that the variety of the control system must be as great as the variety of the inputs to be controlled. As Neil (1969) puts it, it is only possible for the individual learner to exploit his talents 'if the variety of the control system available to the teacher matches the variety of the group of learners in his charge'.

III.8 Equifinality

It is evident in education that equifinality is an important concept in the design of the instructional process, since as teachers, we are attempting to train pupils to achieve certain goals or objectives. It should be remembered, however, that these objectives may be achieved by learners whose initial attainments are very different from each other, and who will reach the objectives by a variety of different routes. In designing the system, it is not homogeneity of treatment which is important but the effectiveness of the various treatments that may be used to enable pupils with different sets of characteristics to achieve the same goals. There is a danger, as some suggest, that increased organizational effectiveness in schools will produce stereotyping of pupil treatments.

IV. SOME PRACTICAL APPLICATIONS OF A SYSTEMS APPROACH IN A SECONDARY SCHOOL

In a paper of this kind it is impossible to do more than outline ways in which general systems theory concepts may be applied to the problems of the organization of the instructional process. One or two examples of ways in which this approach is being implemented in a secondary school in Glasgow may help to suggest further lines of enquiry (Hodge, 1969b).

Apart from the need for a detailed analysis of the components and structures of the teaching-learning process, one of the immediate problems facing teachers in a comprehensive system of education is the variety of pupil entry behaviours at the input stage. This problem is made more difficult by the trend towards what in Scotland is termed a 'common course' - that is, the system whereby setting or streaming is left, in theory at least, until the end of the first or even the second year of the secondary school. While the idea of eliminating the socially undesirable effects of selection at 11+ is to be welcomed, there appears to be a danger that the measures used previously to provide teachers with some diagnosis of pupil abilities will cease to be used and that this, albeit inadequate, source of information will be lost, because of the association in the minds of some people that tests necessarily involve the idea of selection.

This year an attempt was made to diagnose attainment on entry in two major subject areas - English and arithmetic. The tests chosen for this were the English Progress Test D and the Barnard Number Test 1 which are published by the National Foundation for Educational Research. Both tests were administered by the staff in the school who adhered strictly to the instructions for administration. The results are shown in the following figures (Figures 5, 6 and 7). One or two points of interest emerged.

(1) Differences were found between the mean class scores of the various classes on the arithmetic test, although these did not appear to be as marked in the case of the English progress test.

(2) The problem of the variety of pupil input is highlighted by an examination of the distributions for the various classes on each of the two tests. Classes 1A, 1B, and 1C, which were streamed on the basis of IQ scores of 115 and over show a typically negative skew towards the upper limit of the scale, while the remaining four classes which were randomly assigned on the basis of sex present very similar distributions which are normal or near-normal. Obviously, the organizational problems arise when trying to provide courses for the latter groups where the variety is greatest.

Perhaps more interesting and of more immediate practical value to teachers is the analysis of specific deficiencies and difficulties as shown up by item analysis. It should be added that not all the errors shown in the graphs can be attributed to differences in attainment: some items of the tests themselves appear to require revision. But what is interesting is the possible application of this technique with the help of a computer for the rapid diagnosis of initial pupil deficiencies and the printing out of decisions about the specific areas where pupils require remedial treatment before they can embark on a course. Similar decision structures based on

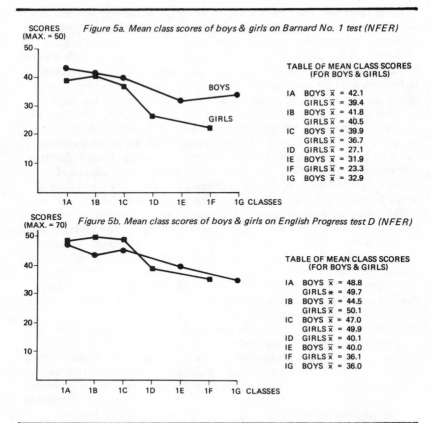

SCORES (MAX. = 50)

Figure 5a. Mean class scores of boys & girls on Barnard No. 1 test (NFER)

BOYS

GIRLS

TABLE OF MEAN CLASS SCORES
(FOR BOYS & GIRLS)

IA	BOYS $\bar{x}$ =	42.1
	GIRLS $\bar{x}$ =	39.4
IB	BOYS $\bar{x}$ =	41.8
	GIRLS $\bar{x}$ =	40.5
IC	BOYS $\bar{x}$ =	39.9
	GIRLS $\bar{x}$ =	36.7
ID	GIRLS $\bar{x}$ =	27.1
IE	BOYS $\bar{x}$ =	31.9
IF	GIRLS $\bar{x}$ =	23.3
IG	BOYS $\bar{x}$ =	32.9

1A 1B 1C 1D 1E 1F 1G CLASSES

SCORES (MAX. = 70)

Figure 5b. Mean class scores of boys & girls on English Progress test D (NFER)

TABLE OF MEAN CLASS SCORES
(FOR BOYS & GIRLS)

IA	BOYS $\bar{x}$ =	48.8
	GIRLS $*$ =	49.7
IB	BOYS $\bar{x}$ =	44.5
	GIRLS $\bar{x}$ =	50.1
IC	BOYS $\bar{x}$ =	47.0
	GIRLS $\bar{x}$ =	49.9
ID	GIRLS $\bar{x}$ =	40.1
IE	BOYS $\bar{x}$ =	40.0
IF	GIRLS $\bar{x}$ =	36.1
IG	BOYS $\bar{x}$ =	36.0

1A 1B 1C 1D 1E 1F 1G CLASSES

different error levels have already been used by Stolurow and others using computers, and the system described by Eraut (1969) provides for similar variable input situations. The important point in this type of approach is the validity of the original measures: if you put garbage in, you will get garbage out.

The next stage is to devise within subject measures for each stage in the courses in each subject department. This will require considerable time and energy. This year we are planning to develop a number of short, specialised programmes to remedy some of the major areas of deficiencies identified on the tests already used.

One other small-scale study with a group of first year pupils suggested that one method of overcoming problems of pupil hetero-geneity of attainment might be the use of programmed materials for teaching basic prerequisite knowledge of a kind essential to a course Hodge (1969c). A programme in geographical concepts basic to a first year course was used with a group of 24 first year pupils. The

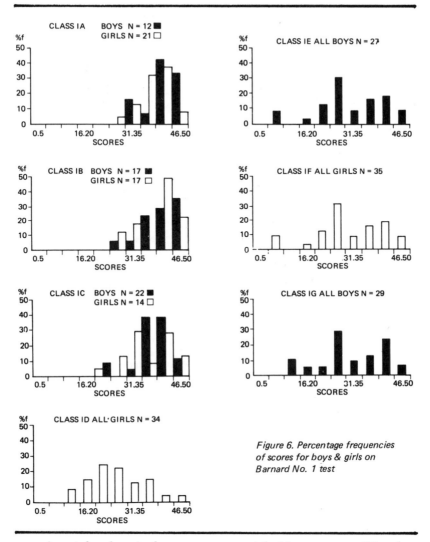

Figure 6. Percentage frequencies
of scores for boys & girls on
Barnard No. 1 test

experimental and control groups were matched by age, sex, IQ and pre-test scores. On analysis, it appeared that there was a mean difference between boys and girls in the two groups on the Pre-Test of approximately 20%, while the two groups, when dichotomised by sex, were perfectly matched. At the end of the programme both groups were given the post-test which was identical to that administered prior to the programme. The programme group also received a 50-item objective test in the class examination at the end of the term. Within the limitations of this experiment, it appears that suitable

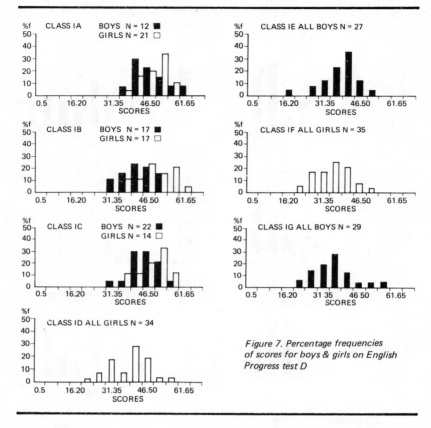

Figure 7. Percentage frequencies of scores for boys & girls on English Progress test D

programmes may help to eliminate, or at least reduce, variations in pupil entry attainments and provide a means of ensuring that all pupils possess the basic knowledge needed prior to the commencement of a course.

CONCLUSION

The application of general systems theory to the organization of the instructional system in secondary schools would appear to hinge on a number of practical problems. The first is the validity of the types of models used to describe the process, and the degree of quantification required in order to test the models. It is suggested that iconic models of the kind described here may be useful initially to describe the sequence of information and energy flows between the various sub-systems. Symbolic models capable of verification would appear to be restricted to those parts of the system which represent specific operations where a high degree of control can be achieved.

The degree of control and quantification possible will in turn depend upon the ability or otherwise of educators to define the system goals in terms of the hierarchies of learning tasks involved and the precise description of the short-term objectives at each stage, as well as upon the measuring instruments and quantification techniques available. Such techniques as probability and set theory, stochastic methods, queueing techniques, games and decision theory would appear to be possible sources for improving predictions about system behaviour.

There is a danger, as Whyte (1957) pointed out, that in our efforts to improve the effectiveness of the system we delude ourselves into thinking that we can create an exact science of man. On the other hand, systems theory and systems analysis may help us to identify more clearly those aspects of learning and teaching which can be controlled more effectively for the benefit of the learner as well as those areas where the creative and artistic talents of the individual should be given free rein.

REFERENCES

1 ACKOFF, R. L
  Systems, organizations and inter-disciplinary research
  'General Systems Yearbook Vol 5 (1960) pp 1-8

2 ASHBY, W. R
  An Introduction to Cybernetics
  London: Chapman & Hall, 1956

3 BEER, S
  Cybernetics and Management
  London: Methuen, 1959

4 BERTALANFFY, L von
  The Theory of Open Systems in Physics and Biology
  Science Vol III (1950) pp 23-29

5 BERTALANFFY, L von
  An Outline of General System Theory
  Brit J Phil Sci Vol I (1950/51) pp 134-65

6 BERTALANFFY, L von
  Problems of Life: An Evaluation of Modern Biological Thought
  New York: J Wiley, 1952

7   CHORLEY, R. J
    Models in Geomorphology
    In: Chorley, R J & Haggett, P (eds) 'Models in Geography'
    London: Methuen, 1967

8   CHORLEY, R. J and HAGGETT, P (eds)
    Models in Geography
    London: Methuen, 1967

9   COOMBS, P. H
    The World Educational Crisis: A Systems Analysis
    New York: Oxford University Press, 1968

10 COULSON, J. E and SILBERMAN, H. F
    Automated Teaching and Individual Differences
    Audio-vis Commun Rev Vol 9, pp 5-15, 1961

11 ERAUT, M. R
    The Design of Variable Input Learning Systems
    In: Dunn, W. R & Holroyd, C (eds) Aspects of Educational
    Technology Volume 2
    London: Methuen, pp 91-99, 1969

12 GEORGE, F
    The Use of Models in Science
    In: Chorley, R J & Haggett, P (1967) op cit

13 HALL, A. D and FAGEN, R. E
    Definition of System
    General Systems Yearbook Vol 1 (1956) pp 18-28

14 HODGE, H. P. R
    A Proposed Model for Investigating the Instructional Process:
    the relationship between learning theory and educational practice
    In: Tobin, M J (ed) Problems and Methods in Programmed
    Learning
    Birmingham: School of Education, University of Birmingham,
    pp 24-51, 1967

15 HODGE, H. P. R
    A Systems Approach to Education: Cyclical Systems in Teaching
    In: Dunn, W R & Holroyd, C (eds) Aspects of Educational
    Technology Volume 2
    London: Methuen, pp 179-190, 1969a

16   HODGE, H. P. R
Systems Analysis and Design in Education: Analogue or Analogy?
Scottish Education Studies Volume 1, No. 3 (June) pp 47-57, 1969b

17   HODGE, H. P. R
Report on the Use of a Linear Programme in Geography with First
Year Pupils in a Secondary School as a Means of Reducing
Heterogeneity of Attainment
Bulletin of the Glasgow University PL Research Unit
Autumn 1969, pp 30-33, 1969c

18   HOYLE, E
How Does the Curriculum Change?
1. A Proposal for Inquiries
J Curric Studies Vol 1 No. 2 (May) pp 132-141, 1969

19   KATZ, D and KAHN, R. L
The Social Psychology of Organizations
New York: J Wiley, 1966

20   MCMILLAN, C and GONZALEZ, R. F
Systems Analysis: A Computer Approach to Decision Models
Homewood, Ill: Richard D Irwin Inc, 1965

21   MILLER, J. G
Living Systems: Basic Concepts
Behavioural Science Vol 10 pp 193-237, 1965

22   NEIL, M. W
An Operational and Systems Approach to Research Strategy in
Educational Technology, (in press), 1969

23   PASK, G
An Approach to Cybernetics
London:Hutchinson, 1961

24   PRIGOGINE, I
Etude Thermodynamique des Phenomenes Irreversibles
Paris: Durrod, 1947

25   SILVERN, L. C
Systems Approach - What Is It?
Educ Technol Vol VIII No. 16 (Aug 30) pp 5-6, 1968a

26 SILVERN, L. C
A Cybernetic System Model for Occupational Education
Educ Technol Vol VIII No. 3 (Jan 30) pp 3-9, 1968b

27 SHANNON, C and WEAVER, W
The Mathematical Theory of Communication
Urbana, Ill: University of Illinois, 1949

28 SMALLWOOD, R. D
A Decision Structure for Teaching Machines
Cambridge, Mass: Massachusetts Institute of Technology Press,
1962

29 STOLUROW, L. M
A Model and Cybernetic System for Research on the Teaching-
Learning Process
Prog Learning Vol 2 No. 3 (October) pp 138-157, 1965

30 WHYTE, W. H
The Organization Man
London: Jonathan Cape, 1957

Contributors

Instructor Commander R E B BUDGETT MA(Cantab) Royal Navy, is the Officer in Charge of the Royal Naval Programmed Instruction Unit and is responsible to the Director General, Personal Services and Training (Navy) in the Ministry of Defence for advice and training in Training System Design and Programmed Instruction.

He was one of the original officers appointed to the RNPIU on its formation in July 1966 to develop the work in Programmed Instruction started by Admiralty Psychologists in 1962. He has been a member of APLET since 1966.

Professor Frank GEORGE is Director of the Institute of Cybernetics at Brunel University.

His interests are broad and especially include semantics, logic, cognitive models and all forms of computer applications especially those concerned with cybernetics. He has a specialist interest also in brain models and artificial intelligence.

Since 1964 he has been computer consultant to Nato, he is Chairman of the Institution of Computer Sciences, The Bureau of Information Science and Honywill George Ltd. The latter two are management and computer consultancy companies. Professor George has published a large number of books and scientific papers, the best known being "The Brain as a Computer" (1961), "Cybernetics and Biology" (1965) and "Models of Thinking" (1970).

Peter HODGE is a graduate of St. Andrews University where he took an Hons. M.A. in Classics. After training for teaching, he worked as a Research Assistant at Aberdeen University developing medical programmes for undergraduates and nurses. Since 1966 he has been in charge of the Programmed Learning Research Unit at Jordanhill College, Glasgow, training teachers in the construction and use of programmes, as well as carrying out research into the use of systems approaches in schools.

Instructor Lieutenant Commander S L MORSE MA, BSc, BEd
Canadian Forces, served an exchange with the Royal Navy from 1968
to 1970 as Training Officer of the Royal Naval Programmed Instruction
Unit. His previous task in Canada had been supervising teams carrying out task analysis for deriving behavioural objectives and subsequent Trade Training Standards for Naval Tradesmen in the
Canadian Forces.

He was trained as an Instructional Programmer with the USAF
Training Systems Division, Lackland Air Force Base, in 1964 and
has been an active member of the NSPI in North America. While in
the United Kingdom he has supported two APLET National Conferences
with papers.

Dr Michael W NEIL was Reader in Biochemistry in the University of
London when he left the academic world in 1965 to join an operational
research consultancy, Science in General Management Ltd. In June
1969 Dr. Neil was Head of Educational Development in the New
Enterprises Division of I.P.C. and in that year left with two of his
colleagues to found Instructional Systems Associates - a consultancy
partnership specialising in a systems approach to education and
training. At present the partners of ISA are deeply involved with the
innovatory work being carried out at the Open University.

Dr Gordon PASK has for many years been involved in research into
and practical applications of cybernetics. One of his main interests
is the application of cybernetics to industrial and military training.

He is Director of Research at System Research Ltd. and Professor
in The Institute of Cybernetics, Brunel University.

Alexander J ROMISZOWSKI MA, DipEd studied engineering and
education at Oxford, thus inevitably becoming involved with industrial
training and particularly with research into training methods.

Since 1964 he has written many instructional programmes, some
published, many more for industrial clients. He is also the author of
a book "The Selection and Use of Teaching Aids" (Kogan-Page) which
attempts to apply a systems approach to lesson planning.

He is currently Deputy Director of the Programmed Instruction
Centre at Enfield College of Technology.

Lieutenant Commander P M STEVENSON Royal Navy, is an Air Engineer, who is also a pilot. Like many Naval Officers his appointments alternate between operational Squadron duties and training. While serving on the staff of the Naval Air Mechanic Training Project. He received his training in Training Analysis and Instructional Programming in the Royal Naval Programmed Instruction Unit.

Edgar STONES BA, MA(Education), PhD is Lecturer in Education (Psychology) at the University of Birmingham. He is also Research Officer of the Colleges of Education Research Group, University of Birmingham, and is the author of several books including:
An Introduction to Educational Psychology, Methuen.
Learning and Teaching: A Programmed Introduction, Wiley.
Readings in Educational Psychology: Learning and Teaching, Methuen.
Towards Evaluation: Some Thoughts on Tests and Teacher Education, Educational Review, Occasional Paper No. 4.